GROWING UP
AS THE
SCAPEGOAT
TO
NARCISSISTIC PARENTS

JAY REID, LPCC

Copyright © 2023 by Jay Reid

All rights reserved. No part of this publication may be reproduced, stored in any form of retrieval system or transmitted in any form or by any means without prior permission in writing from the publishers except for the use of brief quotations in a book review.

Published in the United States of America

Dedication

I dedicate this book to fellow scapegoat survivors of narcissistic abuse.

I would like to thank those who have left comments on my YouTube videos and blog posts. You helped convince me that I could write a book that would be useful to survivors.

I would also like to thank Roger Segalla, Susan Badger, Robert Schulte and Stephen Seligman for their help in my own journey towards healing.

Contents

Dedication iii

Introduction 15
    The Scapegoat Child to a Narcissistic Parent 17
    How Does Narcissism Begin? 19
    When a Narcissist Becomes a Parent 21
    What It Means to Be the Scapegoat Child 22
    When Feeling Close is More Important Than Feeling Good
    23
    Recovery for Scapegoat Survivors 24
    A Guide to Recovery 26
        Pillar #1: Make Sense of What Happened 27
        Pillar #2: Gain Distance from the Narcissistic Abuser 28
        Pillar #3: Defy the Narcissist's Rules 29

Pillar #1: Make Sense of What Happened 31

Chapter 1: The Narcissistic Parent's Fragile Yet Inflated Self-Esteem 32
    The Narcissist's Core Sense of Worthlessness 33
    Two Narcissistic Deficits: Lack of Empathy and Remorse . 33
    How a Narcissist Copes with Their Worthlessness 34
        Denial 34
        Insisting on the Opposite 34
        Feeling Entitled to Special Treatment 35
    When These Strategies Fail 35
    The Narcissistic Parent 36

  Case Examples 37

Chapter 2: Why a Narcissistic Parent Cannot Stand Their Child's Happiness 38

  Happiness in Healthy Relationships 38

  The Narcissist's Drive to Destroy Your Happiness 39

  Why Narcissists Are So Domineering 41

  Your Happiness Threatens the Narcissist's Dominance 43

  Who the Narcissist Chooses to Dominate 43

Chapter 3: The Pressure to Believe What the Narcissistic Parent Says 45

  How Pathological Projective Identification (PPI) Works ... 46

  Why PPI Works 48

    The Need to Share a Reality with a Parent 48

    The Parent's Certainty 50

    The Parent's Intrusiveness 51

  The Need to Identify with the Parent's Unwanted Feelings 52

Chapter 4: The Narcissistic Parent's Rage 54

  What Is Narcissistic Rage? 54

  Why Does a Narcissistic Parent Get Enraged? 56

  Can the Child Avoid the Narcissistic Parent's Rage? 58

  The Impact of Narcissistic Rage on the Child 59

    Learning to Freeze and Submit to Survive 59

    The Four Responses to Trauma 59

  How Shame and Self-Loathing Can Be Adaptive 60

Chapter 5: Why a Narcissist Plays Nice in Public and Abuses in Private 63

Chapter 6: The Altruistic Narcissist 67

Using "Altruism" for the Narcissist's Purposes 68
Why the Altruistic Narcissist Must Hide Their Selfishness . 70
Four Signs of an Altruistic Narcissist 71
    Very Low Patience 71
    Constant Expectation of Gratitude 72
    The Desire to Enforce Rules 73
    "Lost Cause" Friends and Partners 73

Chapter 7: The Enabler Parent 79
What the Enabler's Underprotection Looks Like 80
The Enabler's Psychology 84

Chapter 8: The Scapegoat Child 86
Why a Narcissistic Family Scapegoats a Child 87
What Makes a "Good" Scapegoat 89
The Hellish Life of the Scapegoat Child 91
Common Beliefs of Adults Scapegoated as Children 92
    I Am Physically Disgusting 92
    If I Am Not Being Productive, I Am Worthless 93
    I Am Always One Mistake Away from Complete Ruin .. 94
    I Am Defective 94
    I Have No Skills or Talents 95
    If I Disagree, I Will Be Hated and Exiled 95

Chapter 9: How a Narcissistic Family Scapegoats a Child 98
Convince the Scapegoat Child That They Can Do Nothing Right 99
Convince the Scapegoat Child That They Do Not Deserve What Other Kids Deserve 100
Get the Scapegoat Child to Associate Closeness with There Being Something Wrong 101

Chapter 10: The Scapegoat's Confusion 104
   Why It Can Be Hard to Believe Yourself over the Narcissistic Abuser 104

Chapter 11: The Scapegoat's Mental Frame 109
   Why It Can Feel So Bad to Do What You're Good At 110

Chapter 12: The Worst Parts About Being the Scapegoat 112
   Loneliness and Unloveability 113
   Hopelessness 115

Chapter 13: Narcissistic Abuse Means Always Having to Say You're Sorry 118
   The Fallacy That It Is Always the Scapegoat Child's Fault 119
   How Apologizing Protects the Scapegoat 120
   When the Narcissistic Abuser Tells You That You Don't Really Mean It 121

Chapter 14: Feeling Unreal After Narcissistic Abuse 123
   Recognition Helps Us Feel Real 124
      How It Is Supposed to Work 124
      How It Is Not Supposed to Work 125
   Mirroring and Idealization in the Healthy Family 126
   What Happens in a Narcissistic Family 128
      The "Black Mirror" for the Scapegoat Child of the Narcissist 128
   Having to Falsely Idealize a Narcissistic Parent 130

Chapter 15: Surviving Narcissistic Abuse in Childhood 133
   The Scapegoat Child Is All Alone 134
   Leaving Oneself 135

    The Narcissistic Parent Seeks to Poison the Child's Self-Regard 137

Chapter 16: Shaming the Scapegoat for Having Needs 140

    Why a Narcissistic Abuser Shames the Scapegoat Child for Having Needs 140

    Three Reasons a Narcissistic Parent Turns Your Needs Against You 142

        Your Needs Interfere with Their Needs 142

        Your Needs Remind Them of What They Do Not Have to Give 143

        Your Needs Remind Them of Their Own Dependency on Others 143

Chapter 17: Gratitude as a Survival Strategy 145

    How the Scapegoat Child's Gratitude Is Adaptive 146

Chapter 18: Getting Robbed of Self-Worth 148

    Lack of Recognition 149

    How the Scapegoat Is Denied Recognition for Their Efforts 150

    When Shame Interferes with Recognition 152

Chapter 19: The Power of Language 154

    The Importance of Language 155

    The No-Win Situation 157

Chapter 20: Splitting 159

    Where Does Therapy Pick Up for the Scapegoat Survivor of Narcissistic Abuse? 160

    What Can Therapy Do for the Scapegoat Survivor's Split? 162

Pillar #2: Gain Distance from the Narcissistic Abuser 164

Chapter 21: The Importance of Getting Away from a Narcissistic Abuser 165

    The Forces at Play in a Narcissistically Abusive System ... 166

Chapter 22: Gaining Distance Versus Avoidance 170

    What There Is to Gain 171

    Why Distance from a Narcissistic Abuser Is Self-Care 172

    Guilt: The Sticking Point 173

Chapter 23: The Journey of the Scapegoat Survivor of Narcissistic Abuse 175

    Phase One of the Scapegoat's Journey 176

    Phase Two of the Scapegoat's Journey.............................. 178

Chapter 24: Moving Out of the Narcissistic Parent's Home . 179

    The Narcissistic Parent's Psychological Need to Dominate the Scapegoat Child 180

    How the Narcissistic Parent Coerces the Scapegoat Child to Submit to Their Control... 182

    The Dangers of Moving Out for the Scapegoat Adolescent 182

    How to Protect Yourself When Moving Out 183

Chapter 25: What to Do after Creating Distance from a Narcissistic Abuser... 185

    Lack of Closure with the Narcissistic Abuser.................... 186

    Filling the Vacuum Left by the Narcissist 188

Chapter 26: Safety First: The Secret to Processing Narcissistic Abuse Trauma 190

    Do You Have to Feel Worse before You Can Feel Better? 193

Chapter 27: Moving toward Safe People 197

How to Find Safe People and Move Away from Unsafe People 199
A Sample Checklist of Who's Safe and Who's Not 199
The Challenge of Moving Away from Unsafe People for Scapegoat Survivors 200
The Challenge of Moving toward Safe People for Scapegoat Survivors 201

Chapter 28: Breaking Free of the Trauma Bonds of Narcissistic Abuse 203
Trauma Bonds between the Scapegoat Survivor and the Narcissistically Abusive Parent 204
Trauma Bonds versus Attachment Bonds 205
Trauma Bonds in Movies: *Gone Baby Gone* 206
Strategies to Break the Trauma Bond 208

Chapter 29: The Scapegoat's Instinct to Include Others 209
Why the Scapegoat Survivor Feels Inclusive of Others 210
The Challenge of Being Inclusive When It Comes to Recovery 211

Chapter 30: How to Overcome Guilt after Leaving a Narcissistic Abuser 213
Where the Guilt Comes From 214
Making the Narcissist Happy with You 214
The Narcissistic Abuser's Happiness Takes the Place of Your Own 215
How to Overcome Guilt When Leaving Your Narcissistic Abuser 216
Know That Your Guilt Comes from Feeling Responsible for Someone Else 216
Connect to Safe People and Communities 217

Know You Deserve Your Own Patience and Compassion 217

Chapter 31: Giving up the Quest to Be Important to the Narcissist 218

    How the Quest to Be Important to the Narcissist Begins ... 219

    How to Surrender the Quest 219

    Are You Caught Trying to Be Important to a Narcissist? .. 220

Chapter 32: Giving up the Quest to Prove the Narcissist Wrong About You 222

    The Quest to Prove the Narcissist Wrong 223

Pillar #3: Defy the Narcissist's Rules 229

Chapter 33: Measure the Long Road to Recovery 230

    How Early Did the Narcissistic Abuse Start? 231

    Did Anyone Protect You from the Narcissistic Abuse? 233

    How Long Did the Narcissistic Abuse Last? 234

Chapter 34: Reclaim What You Sacrificed 236

Chapter 35: Fight for Your Right to Have Fun 243

    Why It Can Be Dangerous to Have Fun Around Your Narcissistic Abuser 244

    How to Feel Safe to Have Fun Again 246

Chapter 36: Reclaim Your Voice 247

    Are Relationships All about the Other Person's Needs? 249

    The Role of Shame in Muzzling the Scapegoat Survivor's Voice 250

    How to Remove the Muzzle 251

Chapter 37: Recover Your Confidence 253

    The Danger of Self-Confidence for the Scapegoat Child .. 253

Obstacles to Self-Confidence for Survivors of Narcissistic Abuse 254

Conditions That Can Help You Feel Safer Being Self-Confident Today 255

    Build Relationships with People Who Are Not Narcissistic 255

    Put Distance Between Yourself and the Narcissistic Abuser 256

    Experiment with Ways of Living with Confidence 256

Commit to the Confident Acts 256

Chapter 38: Go from Human *Doing* to Human *Being* 259

Why the Scapegoat Survivor of Narcissistic Abuse Is Pressured to Think More than to Be 260

What Happens when Scapegoated Children Have to Move toward Their Thought-Of Identity 261

Why the Scapegoat Has Had to Overidentify with Their Thought-Of Identity 262

How to Unidentify with the Thought-Of Identity and Increase Connection to Your Being 265

Chapter 39: Learn How to Trust 266

A Narcissistic Parent Leaves the Child Emotionally Malnourished 267

Three Tools to Facilitate Trust After Narcissistic Abuse .. 268

Chapter 40: Know You Are Adequate 270

The Importance of Safe People in Knowing Your Adequacy 274

Chapter 41: Learn How to Talk to Others About a Narcissistic Parent... 275

Narcissistic Parents Often Present a Different Picture to the Public 277

Bring the "Bad" Parent out from behind the Closed Doors of Your Own Mind 277

Chapter 42: Protect Your Right to Success 280

When Feeling Put Down Is Familiar 281

When the Scapegoat Child Is Met with Envy Outside of the Narcissistic Family 281

Protect Yourself from Others' Envy and Devaluation 283

Chapter 43: Decide How You're Spoken To 285

How a Narcissistic Parent Offends from the Victim Position 287

How You Can Choose the Way You Are Treated Now ... 288

Chapter 44: Recover Your Status 290

Why It Is Necessary for the Narcissist to See You as Lower Status 291

The Impact of Being Seen as Lower Status for the Scapegoat Child 292

How to Recover Your Status 293

Chapter 45: Trust What the Narcissist Shows You, Not What You Hope to See 295

The Self-Centered World of Narcissistic Parenting 296

Unlearning the Narcissist: Empowering Yourself after Abuse 299

Overcoming Anxiety: The Path to Self-Assertion 300

Chapter 46: Show Off 302

Why Showing Off Feels So Bad for the Scapegoat Survivor of Narcissistic Abuse 303

    Why the Narcissistic Parent Cannot Stand Your Showing Off 306

Chapter 47: Stop Self-Punishment 307

    Why Scapegoat Survivors Punish Themselves after Good Things Happen 307

    Transform the Practice of Self-Punishment 309

Chapter 48: Seven Self-Care Tools to Help You Defy the Narcissist's Rules 311

    Self-Care Tool #1: Practicing Patience with Yourself 312

    Self-Care Tool #2: Practicing Gratitude toward Yourself . 313

    Self-Care Tool #3: Use Your Breath 313

    Self-Care Tool #4: Making Sure to Move 314

    Self-Care Tool #5: Eating as an Act of Care toward Yourself 315

    Self-Care Tool #6: The Respect Survey 316

    Self-Care Tool #7: How the Well-Adjusted World Sees You 317

References 319

Introduction

At age twenty-two, I found myself in a therapy session. Along with the other new students in my clinical psychology program, I had been advised to seek personal therapy as part of my training. My hope was that going to graduate school would win me the relief I so needed. But relief from what? I wasn't sure. I knew that there had been an element of struggle to each moment of my existence for as long as I could remember. If I could succeed in graduate school, maybe life wouldn't feel like such a battle. Maybe I would feel like what I thought, felt, and said mattered. Maybe I would overcome the nagging feeling that I was somehow defective.

So here I was, ready to be told what was wrong with me so that I could start fixing myself, be "cleansed," and finally get to matter.

"So, tell me about what it was like in your family growing up," my therapist prompted.

I told her my father had seemed wholly disinterested in who I was as a person. In contrast, my mother had been very easy to talk to, and I'd felt much closer to her. She had died from cancer a year earlier. "The weird thing is," I continued, "I didn't feel anything when she died. No sadness. Nothing. I don't know what's wrong with me. How could I not feel grief over my own mother passing?"

My therapist looked at me intently. "What was it like when your mother would get angry or upset?"

"Oh, then all bets were off. She'd scream at me at the top of her lungs. She looked like she wanted to kill me. But that was just because I was such a bad kid."

"Really? What made you such a bad kid?" she asked.

"Well, I got caught drinking in the tenth grade and got arrested. That was the big thing. But then it was a lot of little things. Like, I wouldn't remember to take the trash out a lot of the time. Or I was always trying to get out of doing chores. I just was not responsible as a kid. And I was selfish. I cared more about being with my friends than I did about being with my family. My mom always had to get on me about that. I shouldn't have been so shallow—caring more about being popular than being a good son."

"Would your mother tell you such things?"

"Oh yeah! She'd tell me I was immature, irresponsible, and selfish. Seemed like I was always being selfish in her eyes. That hurt the most, but I guess I deserved it."

"Why do you say you deserved it?"

"Because she wouldn't have yelled at me so much if I hadn't been so bad all the time."

At this, the therapist cocked her head and looked at me. "Did anyone ever stick up for you? Take your side? Or tell you that it wasn't right for a parent to treat you this way?"

I thought about this for a moment. "No. I mean who would've done that? She only yelled at me when we were alone. My dad was not the kind of guy who would get involved. He'd just tell me that my mother loved me and that I needed to figure out a way to get along with her."

"Jay, I want you to know something. What you're describing is not normal. Children are not typically treated this way. It sounds to me like your mother emotionally and verbally abused you on a regular basis. I also think you had to develop some painful ideas about yourself in order to cope, like that you are selfish, or 'bad,' as you put it. I think our therapy might focus on these ideas and helping you eventually trust that they're not—nor have they ever been—true about who you are."

I had been ready to be told that I was the problem, and here my therapist was telling me something entirely different. The problem—as far as I understood it—was that I *thought* I was the problem. And the origins of this new problem seemed to lie in how my mother had treated me and my father ignored me. I was caught off guard and surprised to learn that I might not have deserved her bouts of yelling and cruelty. I didn't quite believe that yet, but I saw a glimmer of an existence that might not be so fraught. Maybe the day would come when I wasn't always blaming myself—the way my family always had—and I could enjoy being who I am.

The Scapegoat Child to a Narcissistic Parent

Mine is one of many stories of children who have survived a childhood of being blamed, devalued, intimidated, punished, and subjected to harsh restriction by a narcissistic parent. I was the scapegoat child to a narcissistic mother. I had no other adult in the family who was able or willing to step in to protect me. I had to conclude that I deserved my narcissistic mother's belittling and blame. I could not let myself see that

I had been mistreated until she passed away and I was in my therapist's office.

The term scapegoat comes from the Old Testament. In preparation for the Day of Atonement, or Yom Kippur, the Jewish people performed a ritual involving two goats. One of the goats was subject to sacrificial slaughter, while the members of the community pinned their sins upon the other. That second goat was then cast into exile in a rocky headland away from the village, taking the sins with it. It became known as the scapegoat.

The notion of sin is useful in understanding the experience of the child marked as the scapegoat by a narcissistic family. Most scapegoat survivors carry with them an indelible and long-held sense that they are guilty, dirty, bad, undeserving of leniency, and incapable of innocence. They feel like they are full of sin, while those around them are blameless, superior, innocent, and much more deserving. When the scapegoat child is cast as the sinner, the rest of the family gets to be cast as saints. Of course there is a manipulation of reality going on: the scapegoat child is not really to blame for everyone else's sins, but that's what the majority insists upon.

The term "scapegoat" reflects the way my mother treated me as well as the role I had to assume to stay a member of my family. In other words, scapegoat can be used as a verb and an adjective. The word captures what a narcissistic parent does to a child and the painful role the child must inhabit to survive.

How Does Narcissism Begin?

Someone who is narcissistic has a fragile yet inflated view of their own self-worth, and requires other people to keep it intact. This way of being can stem from early life experiences. The field of psychoanalysis[1] has contributed important insights into this psychological condition.

Heinz Kohut and his form of psychoanalysis—known as "self psychology"—argues that narcissism develops as the result of insufficient and inconsistent parental responsiveness. This understanding of the narcissistic person is a sympathetic one. Kohut observed that young children have an outsized belief in their own capacities or grandiosity. Simultaneously, they are particularly vulnerable, and need for their caregivers to realistically and consistently nurture this belief. No parent is perfect, so the child is bound to feel missed at one point or another. But if that is the exception and not the rule, the child learns to trust that the parent intends to—and will—return to affirming the child when needed. The child puts these nurturing experiences into their psychology. During this process, the child's grandiosity gets transformed into a realistic and ongoing basis for self-esteem.

---

[1] Psychoanalysis is a long-term form of therapy. Its goal is to get the client's way of organizing reality to reveal itself in the relationship to the therapist so that change can happen. It typically involves meeting three to five times per week. Work done by therapists, researchers, and theorists in this discipline has produced important insights about what a person needs to love and work successfully in life, what happens when we do not get what we need, and how that can be addressed to resume development gone awry.

A child can be at risk of developing narcissistic personality disorder if they are consistently deprived of the needed nurturing responsiveness from their parents. In these cases, the child is not offered the kinds of affirmation they need to internalize a sense of their own worth and abilities. Their grandiosity does not transform into a realistic basis for self-esteem. They persist in their grandiose expectations regarding themselves and others' responses to them. As they become older, gain more influence in the world, and have people who are dependent on them, they can coerce others to reflect their grandiosity. The problem is that the lack of receiving this from their parents has created an empty bucket inside that never feels full. The narcissistic adult constantly seeks others' affirmation without it ever modifying their grandiosity.

I will add here that someone who becomes narcissistic typically cannot empathize with others nor reflect on themselves in a realistic way. There is a concrete quality to their grandiose perceptions, which they refuse to question. The feelings of others do not seem to emotionally matter to these individuals. As a result, they are typically not the people who show up for therapy. It is more often the people close to them, who possess this ability to empathize and self-reflect, that end up seeking counseling.

Of course, not everyone who lives through such a depriving childhood becomes narcissistic. I have found this to be the case with survivors of narcissistic parents. Somehow, these people retain the ability to reflect on themselves and others in a curious and empathic way. These traits made them vulnerable to the narcissistic parent's exploitation, but the good news is that they also make it possible to heal and eventually enjoy reciprocal relationships with safe people.

When a Narcissist Becomes a Parent

A narcissistic parent's first priority is to keep their fragile yet inflated self-esteem propped up. This mission is difficult, because the narcissist also feels worthless at their core and cannot tolerate these feelings. Instead, they unconsciously deny their self-loathing and consciously insist on the opposite: that they are worth more than other people. Now the narcissist must work around the clock to keep their bad feelings at bay while promoting good feelings. Viewing—and treating—someone else as the loathsome one can be very helpful with this goal.

For a narcissistic parent, their child can be a convenient person to offload these feelings of self-loathing onto. Since the child is dependent on the parent for emotional and physical survival, the parent holds a great deal of leverage in the relationship. If the parent is narcissistic, they may use that leverage to force the child to identify with feelings the narcissistic parent cannot stand in themselves. When this happens, the narcissistic parent is scapegoating their child.

My case is a good example of this. My narcissistic mother generally seemed pleased with herself. I do not recall her expressing self-doubt or self-criticism. At the same time, she never seemed to pass up an opportunity to undermine my belief in myself or criticize my choices, mannerisms, or appearance. Over my years in therapy, my therapist and I pieced together that her cruel treatment of me reflected how hard she was trying to evade her own self-hatred. This understanding was important, not to garner sympathy for her, but to shed light on what was really happening. When she would emotionally and psychologically abuse me, it was not because I deserved it. She mistreated me because she could not tolerate how much she despised herself. As a result, she scapegoated me as the person she could hate instead.

What It Means to Be the Scapegoat Child

In order for the scapegoat child to share a reality with a narcissistic parent intent on using them in this way, the child has to fundamentally believe they deserve the abuse.

The narcissistic parent does not scapegoat a child by saying something honest like, "Oh, I love being mean to you because it makes me feel less bad about myself. I am using you to buffer my own self-hatred. And I have very little empathy for others, so your hurt feelings mean nothing to me."

Instead, the parent tends to "offend from the victim position." They frame the child as having committed a horrendous offense that supposedly justifies the parent's abusive behavior.

So, a narcissistic parent's ploy would look more like walking into a room and seeing their five-year old son's toy on the floor. They might exclaim to him, "What is this? What is this?! I told you to pick up your toys, and I almost tripped over this and hurt myself. What is wrong with you? Why can't you do what I tell you to do?" Next, the parent might grab the child harshly by the arm and briskly walk him to his room while yelling, "If you're not going to listen to me, then I am going to just have to make you! You stay in here until you know how to do what I tell you."

The five-year old boy concludes that his mother would not have "had to" yell at him if he had just put his toys away. More globally, if he had just been a better son, she would not have been so mean to him.

It is these kinds of exchanges that lead the scapegoat child to believe they deserve the abuse they receive. When a child is faced with an abusive parent, they must protect their attachment to the parent before they can protect themselves.

Attachment refers to our innate drive to forge emotional bonds with our parents. Children need to feel like their parent is "near"—especially emotionally. When a parent is emotionally close to a child and respectful of that child's autonomy a secure attachment bond can develop.

As the securely attached child matures into an adolescent, they increase their domains of independence. The young person has developed an internal working model of attachment that provides them with an emotional sense of nearness to their parents.

When Feeling Close is More Important Than Feeling Good

In the absence of such good-enough attachment to their parent, the child must scramble to find any sense of secure attachment. When the parent cannot attune to the child's inner world, the child's need for the parent will compel them to abandon their inner world to match that of their parent. Thus, if the parent is treating the child as if they are bad, then the child must believe this to protect the parent's flimsy attachment to them. Children in this situation adopt a stance of heightened compliance toward the parent. Instead of being near the parent, their only choice is to become an extension of the parent.

The scapegoat child will likely have to form a lot of beliefs that serve to convince them that they are the bad person in the relationship with their parent. These beliefs involve being defective and/or undeserving. If the child believes there is something wrong with them, or that they deserve very little, it makes sense to them that their parent finds fault with them or sees them as unimportant.

The beliefs the child has to adopt, and the resulting suffering, is what it means to *be* the scapegoat to the narcissistic parent.

I always felt dissatisfied with myself. During my childhood and adolescence, I had to contend with private debates about my defectiveness as a person. It would be hard to look in the mirror because I hated what I saw. I found it difficult to listen to my voice on recordings. I braced myself whenever someone brought up something I had done in the past, because I was ready for them to find some kind of fault in me. In order to maintain a relationship with my narcissistic mother, I had to believe I was defective. All of these perceptions of myself as an objectionable person were ways in which I complied with this belief.

Recovery for Scapegoat Survivors

Having to serve in the role of scapegoat to a narcissistic parent means having to believe painful things about yourself that are not true. Believing these things makes it possible for the scapegoat child to feel like their parent is on their side. For example, "Mom and Dad are on my side because they show me how I am bad so that I can be a better child to them." It is better for the scapegoat child to believe these terrible things about themselves than to acknowledge—as a child—that there is nobody on their side.

As you get older and gain some independence from your narcissistic parent, recovery becomes a possibility. I define recovery as a quality of life where you embrace your existence, know you deserve love just as you are, protect yourself from dangerous people and influences, and connect to a community of people.

At the start of the path toward recovery, these outcomes can seem more like ideas than experience. In this book I offer a map of how to go from being the scapegoat to a narcissistic parent to recovering the quality of life you deserve. Scapegoat survivors of narcissistic parents have had to learn and practice ways of living that discount their value and prioritize the needs of those who mistreat them. They assume they deserve nothing from others. The path toward recovery involves deprogramming this mindset and tuning into what you want from a place of respect and deservedness. This book highlights the steps you can take to get there. It tends to happen over time, and the process of change is incremental. I emphasize exercising compassion and patience toward yourself through this process.

It is important to understand the conditions under which the scapegoat role originated so that you can set up different conditions in your life today as you work to recover and heal. If it felt necessary to believe you were defective and undeserving to maintain important relationships in the past, it will be essential to find and participate in relationships that run on a different kind of fuel. As you get to find, build, and trust relationships with people who see you as deserving and admirable, it will feel emotionally and psychologically safer to challenge the beliefs you had to hold as the scapegoat child.

A Guide to Recovery

In my personal and professional experience in recovering from narcissistic abuse, three defining features have emerged. I present these with the goal of offering a coherent picture of the sometimes complex process of recovery from this form of abuse.

The 3 Pillars of Recovery for Scapegoat Survivors

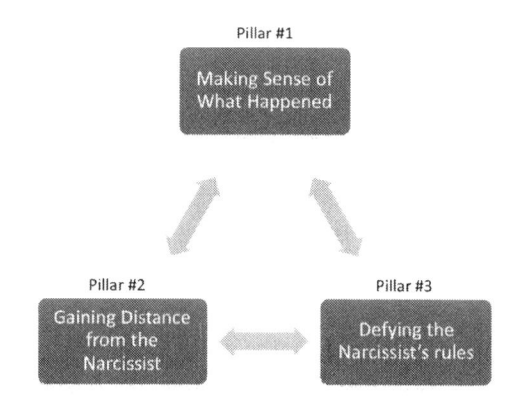

Pillar #1
Making Sense of What Happened

Pillar #2
Gaining Distance from the Narcissist

Pillar #3
Defying the Narcissist's rules

Being the scapegoat child to a narcissistic parent means being estranged from your core sense of self. To paraphrase famous humanistic psychologist Carl Rogers, our core selves warrant our trust and respect for navigating the world (1995). As such, our unique, authentic selves cannot be undeserving and defective, as the narcissistic parent claims.

The idea that the scapegoat survivor is undeserving and defective originates from a lie the narcissistic parent tells in an attempt to prop up their own flagging self-worth. Living as though this lie is true means being separated from your authentic self. As a result, the scapegoat survivor can feel lost and confused as to how to find their way back to who they *really* are in the world.

The three pillars of recovery offer scapegoat survivors a map to help orient them back to their actual selves. The chapters of this book are organized in accordance with these pillars. Let's take a look at what you can expect.

Pillar #1: Make Sense of What Happened

The scapegoat survivor has lived through an attempt to convince them that they were something other than how they seemed to themselves. Gaining an understanding of pathological narcissism and the resulting process of scapegoating can help the survivor begin to challenge the fundamental assumption that they deserved the narcissistic parent's abuse.

As you learn how and why narcissistic parents have to find someone else to devalue in order to keep themselves propped up, you can begin to see the messages you got from your parent in a new light. Instead of assuming your guilt in the face of their accusations that you were defective and/or undeserving, you might begin to wonder if they felt this way about themselves. Such questions allow some light into the mineshaft of being in the role of scapegoat. That light can grow incrementally as you move along your process of recovery.

The first section of this book is dedicated to this pillar. First, the psychology of the narcissistic parent is explained. This information will help you understand that the devaluation and derision you faced as a scapegoat was not about you but about your parent's own psychological disturbance. Next, I address the different ways that narcissistic abuse can show up in the family—from the altruistic narcissist, to the enabler parent, to the scapegoat. Last, I address the inner experience of the scapegoat child. My hope is that you might see some of your own experience reflected here and know you are not alone in this. These chapters emphasize the ways in which the scapegoat's inner experience is a product of how the narcissistic parent mistreated them. Thus, you may feel more justified in finding compassion for yourself in the kinds of inner challenges you have to contend with today. Compassion for oneself is a critical antidote to the abuse suffered in the role of scapegoat.

Pillar #2: Gain Distance from the Narcissistic Abuser

Being the scapegoat to a narcissistic parent means having to adapt to a context where you have to think and experience yourself as lower status than the parent. For members of narcissistic families, the pressure to do this is intense. Even after childhood and adolescence, having an interaction with a narcissistic parent or enabling family member can evoke the scapegoat experience. You may notice feeling more defective or undeserving after such an exchange.

This is why emotional, psychological, and perhaps even physical distance is so important. In order to know at every level of your being that you do not need to continue to believe you are defective or undeserving, you need to remove yourself from relationships that require this of you. In the early phases of recovery, the scapegoat survivor's system is primed to do what used to work to keep the relationship with the narcissistic parent intact. As such, it can be important to limit contact at this stage.

The principle of moving away from your narcissistic parent is an important one to apply. More broadly, this pillar is about moving away from people who are unsafe to you. At the same time, you will focus on moving *toward* safe people.

The second section of this book is dedicated to this pillar explains the importance of gaining distance from the narcissistic abuser. You will learn the qualities of safe people that you might seek in your life and to rely on your own judgement, experience, and to do so. You will also read how to address the obstacles that the scapegoat survivor may encounter when trying to move away from a narcissistic abuser. These obstacles include feelings of guilt, shame, disloyalty, and disorientation.

Pillar #3: Defy the Narcissist's Rules

As you gain insight into the abuse you experienced and create the needed distance from the source of this abuse, the third pillar of recovery emerges. Hopefully, you will come to understand the rules of your narcissistic abuser in the first two sections. This pillar involves living in defiance of those rules.

Beliefs about being defective or undeserving function to make you comply with the narcissist's rules. These rules can take different specific forms but all work to keep the narcissist's fragile yet inflated self-worth intact. Your negative beliefs were adopted to ward off the danger of losing the narcissistic parent's willingness to care for you. In recovery, you will discover relationships where it is safe to act and think of yourself as deserving and intact. This is an important piece to living in defiance of the narcissist's rules. Survivors most effectively do this in connection with other healthy people who endorse such defiance. You will learn that these new relationships are strengthened—not threatened—by you asserting and acting from your worth.

I emphasize the importance of defying the narcissist's rules in new, safe relationships because I believe that survivors *can* find such people. From the perspective of control-mastery theory—which I employ in my own practice—there is good reason to assume that scapegoat survivors are on the lookout for relationships where they can feel safe enough to disconfirm the beliefs they had to adopt earlier (Silberschatz, 2013). Often, this search may be unconscious because our consciousness has to be dominated by such grim beliefs of being undeserving and/or defective.

The third section of this book shows you possibilities for how you can identify and break free from the narcissist's rules. Generally, this process involves seeing the ways in which you have had to artificially put yourself down so that the narcissist could artificially be propped up. Once you understand this process, you'll learn it is safe to challenge it. The role of scapegoat demands that you withhold your full capacities from yourself. Engaging with this pillar of recovery means you get to access, engage, and take credit for those capacities. Each chapter in this section presents a rule that is meant to be broken!

Pillar #1:

Make Sense of What Happened

1

The Narcissistic Parent's Fragile Yet Inflated Self-Esteem

> *Did your parent find your opinions, feelings, and needs to be unimportant?*
> *Did your parent always seem to find something wrong with you?*
> *Did you feel invisible to your parent?*

The psychology of a narcissistic parent is very likely to end in abuse for their children. In this chapter I explain how and why.

Life can feel confusing for a child born into a family headed by a narcissistic mother or father, particularly if that child is the family scapegoat. It can seem like everything the child does is wrong and everything the narcissistic parent does is right. In recovering from childhood narcissistic abuse, it is important to understand the psychology of the narcissistic mother or father. Doing so can allow survivors to finally know the truth of who they actually are in relation to their abusive parent.

The Narcissist's Core Sense of Worthlessness

Narcissistic mothers and fathers suffer an unbearable sense of inadequacy and shame. They believe they are worthless and cannot acknowledge it; doing so feels like it would end in their psychological destruction. As a result, this belief in their own worthlessness is typically denied and split off into their unconscious.

Many scapegoat survivors of narcissistically abusive parents are surprised to learn that the parent who tyrannized them suffered from profound feelings of worthlessness. I believe this stems from how effectively a narcissistic parent can deny and relocate these feelings into the people around them (e.g., the scapegoat child). This defensive process allows the parent to *seem* infallible. Without these other people to suffer *for* them, however, the narcissistic parent may have to feel their own dreaded feelings.

Two Narcissistic Deficits: Lack of Empathy and Remorse

Narcissists are unwilling and/or unable to care about how their actions impact others. Research has generally shown that they lack empathy for the feelings of others (Urbonaviciute & Hepper, 2020). They may be able to read and use others' feelings for their own purposes, but they will not genuinely care about the emotional well-being of someone else.

Additionally, a narcissist is remorseless in whatever they do to prop up their artificial self-worth. Many of my clients with narcissistic parents have had the experience of getting blamed all over again when they've tried to confront that parent about their abusive treatment. The narcissist would rather claim that their child deserved the abuse than take accountability for hurting their child. It simply does not seem to matter to the narcissist, because the feelings of other people do not count nearly as much as their own.

How a Narcissist Copes with Their Worthlessness

Denial

A narcissist tries to solve their feelings of worthlessness by keeping them out of their awareness. Although the associated feelings of shame may be felt and reacted to, the narcissist does not consciously register them. They live in a world where they have to fend off a dreaded sense of inadequacy yet do not have the psychological nor emotional fortitude to know what it is they dread. They must deny these feelings because they seem too threatening.

Insisting on the Opposite

Next, they adopt a conscious belief that is the opposite of feeling worthless: a belief in their own superiority and specialness. In psychology, we call this "grandiosity." Put simply, the narcissist believes their feelings, capabilities, thoughts, and needs are more important than others'. This positive view is meant to combat their sense of worthlessness. It creates demands that others admire, agree with, and welcome the narcissist at all times, or face their wrath. So, the solution they enact is always fragile and vulnerable to disruption.

Feeling Entitled to Special Treatment

The next step involves the narcissist's expectation that others will comply with their inflated self-worth. They unconsciously expect and demand that others reflect back to them how special and full of worth they are. In other words, they feel entitled to constant admiration and prioritization.

The narcissist can experience other people as psychological extensions of themselves. The other person is there to make the narcissist feel superior, and if they fail, the narcissist has no use for them. Children are particularly vulnerable to this. A child cannot bear to be seen as useless by their parent and will typically work very hard to prevent this from happening. As a result, many children of narcissistic parents are familiar with having to provide them with heaping amounts of admiration, agreement, and permission.

When These Strategies Fail

The narcissist's strategies are temporarily effective in alleviating their immediate sense of worthlessness. As with all band-aid approaches, however, they must be in constant operation to achieve the protective effect. These strategies have to work in every situation—otherwise the narcissist's sense of worthlessness could "break through" to awareness. Disruptions often come in the form of other people's needs, differences of opinion, or just failure to notice how "special" the narcissist is.

When someone else expresses a need, the narcissist does not see it as an opportunity to attune to that person and strengthen the bond between them. Instead, they take the expression of the other's need to mean that theirs are not as important. As such, the narcissist may avoid people with enough self-worth to feel deserving of having their needs met. If they cannot avoid someone else with a need—such as their own child—they will employ other strategies to coerce that person to stifle their needs. The narcissist punishes others with needs using common tactics such as: shaming them for being too "needy" or "selfish"; outright neglect; dismissing their needs as illegitimate; and/or accusing them of seeking attention. The goal for the narcissist is to make the person feel worse after expressing a need. Once the other person stops doing so, they no longer challenge the narcissist's belief that their needs are all that should matter in the world.

What if someone fails to cooperate with the narcissist's entitlement to their admiration, agreement, and permission? They can expect to be met with either indignant anger or a cold dismissal. The anger is designed to coerce them into treating the narcissist as special again. However, often when the narcissist does not have influence over the other person, they can instead turn cold, switch off from them. Suddenly the other person does not matter, and the narcissist moves on to people more willing to go along with their inflated sense of importance.

The Narcissistic Parent

The child of a narcissist is almost doomed to mess up the strategies of inflated self-worth and entitlement. By design, a young baby is a bundle of needs. They are entirely dependent on their caregiver and can only offer their continued existence as thanks. For most caregivers, this is more than enough. It is, in fact, why they had a child: to experience the gratification of meeting the needs of someone they love.

For a narcissistic parent, the child may be welcome so long as they reflect back the parent's self-importance. The kid has to orbit the parent. This is unnatural, since children have appropriate developmental needs to experience themselves as the center of the universe and their parents as their satellites. If a child indicates that they expect the narcissistic parent to orbit them, the narcissist will see this as an unforgivable sign of disrespect. As discussed above, such acts can evoke the sense of worthlessness the narcissist is always working to deny. These supposed transgressions are inevitable so long as the kid tries to hold on to their own perspective and needs. The attributes of the narcissistic parent will coerce the kid to relinquish their connection to themselves and find a way to orbit the narcissistic parent.

Case Examples

In this book I make extensive use of case examples to illustrate the dynamics of narcissistic abuse, scapegoating and steps in recovery. These case examples are composites of my personal, professional, and theoretical experience and knowledge. To protect client's confidentiality I have modified all identifying information while leaving the essence of their experience intact.

2

Why a Narcissistic Parent Cannot Stand Their Child's Happiness

> *Do you feel wary and self-conscious when smiling?*
> *Do you play down your achievements so that others don't feel outdone?*
> *Do you have trouble knowing what you excel in?*

One tell-tale sign of having been abused by a narcissist is feeling wary of your own happiness. That may sound strange or odd. Why would anyone shy away from smiling, laughing, getting excited, or feeling vitalized? The answer takes a little explaining but gets to the root of the narcissist's danger to others.

Happiness in Healthy Relationships

As I am writing this, I see a toddler across the room in the café where I am sitting. The boy is wholly occupied with some sort of toy, and his mother watches him with a deep fondness. She glides her fingers over his hair, careful not to disturb his focus. I think it is safe to say that she's happy because her son is happy.

This is a beautiful display of non-possessive love by a mother toward her child. The boy evokes this expression of love from her by doing what makes him happy. Extrapolating from this episode, we might assume that when this boy considers how his mother thinks of him, he might feel warm, special, and worthy of her care. In short, it leaves him feeling loved. Of course, toddlers do not "think" in the same way adults do, but they have ways of knowing how others think of them. This boy is lucky in that his template for how others see him is accurate and positive.

The Narcissist's Drive to Destroy Your Happiness

The notion of non-possessive love does not compute for a narcissist. They insist that everyone else's happiness must go through them. Why? This is where the motivational systems of "normal" people and narcissists differ. Most of us seek mutual connection with the people in our lives. A narcissist's fundamental motivation is to feel superior to, more important than, and in charge of those closest to them. A narcissist wants these people to care more about what the narcissist thinks about them than what they think about themselves.

> Joe was a client who had survived a narcissistic mother. He would recall moments of terror when she asked him if he had done some household chore—inevitably one he had forgotten about. When he told her, "No, I forgot," she launched into a rage. While screaming at the top of her lungs, she accused him of being selfish, inconsiderate, and irresponsible. She would then use the good things he had done earlier against him. "You just want to be the center of attention, but you do

not do anything to actually help this family!" Spittle would spark out of her mouth as her eyes fixed on him, turning black with hate.

The worst part of her attacks was that, if Joe wanted to maintain a relationship with her, he had to agree that he was as terrible as she claimed. A child has to have to have a relationship with their parent, so this was not really a choice for him. Joe's mother had no qualms about exploiting his natural dependency to get her own needs met.

As therapy proceeded, Joe and I figured out that his mother's tirades often came after good moments. See, Joe is naturally funny, charismatic, and caring toward others. When his mother got home from work, he and his sister would go into the kitchen while she made dinner. Joe would playfully tease his sister and joke around with his mother. Her questions about the chores usually came toward the end of the meal.

Joe and I determined that his mother may have felt threatened by his easy ability to connect with and raise the spirits of her and his sister in those moments. We wondered if her participation with Joe in the "fun" before dinner led to her feeling outdone by him. It made sense to Joe that that might make her feel worse about herself. Since her own feelings of inferiority, inadequacy, and the resulting shame were intolerable to her, she had to take them out on her son. By yelling at him for some trumped up offense after dinner, she could devalue him enough that his presence did not remind her of her own worthlessness as much.

As this kind of abuse wore on, Joe developed a very stoic demeanor. With select friends, he might show his humor and vitality, but he generally constrained himself. Although he felt a sense of deadness inside, this tactic spared him his mother's rage at times.

Joe has now recovered much of his liveliness through his own strength and hard work in and out of therapy.

Why Narcissists Are So Domineering

In order to understand why narcissists operate so poisonously in relationships, it is important to understand a little more about how good-enough reciprocal relationships work.

We need others' recognition to become ourselves. Remember the riddle, "If a tree falls in a forest and nobody is there to hear it, does it make a sound?"

Jessica Benjamin explains why the answer would be a resounding "no" when it comes to human development (2013). Without the other's recognition of who we are and what we are doing, thinking, and becoming, we do not feel confirmed in any of those ways of being. For example, if we clap and nobody else hears it, we will not feel like we've made a sound.

Benjamin puts it best:

A person comes to feel that "I am the doer who does, I am the author of my acts," by being with another person who recognizes her acts, her feelings, her intentions, her existence,

> *her independence . . . The subject declares, "I am, I do," and waits for the response, "You are, you have done." (p. 21)*

Importantly, the other has to act and be independent from us. We do not feel truly recognized if we are controlling the other, influencing them to provide us with the recognition. Recognition must be given. It can never be taken. The toddler in the cafe received his mother's recognition as he played with his toy. She gave it to him because she wanted to. Her respect for his focus on the toy showed that she recognized and respected his independence too.

If the other has what we need and we have no absolute control over whether it is given, then our independence rests in our dependence on the other. There is a boldness and a vulnerability in being who we are. Bold because we must act in accord with what we truly feel. Vulnerable because we need the other to be willing to recognize those acts, and we cannot control the other's willingness. We also need that recognition to be able to acknowledge our own independence.

A narcissist rejects this vulnerability. At the deepest of levels, a narcissist has traded recognition from an independent other for dominance over a submissive other. In this kind of arrangement, there is nobody left to truly recognize the narcissist. Although the narcissist forgoes the kind of recognition that would let them feel their real existence, they do get a feeling of power and superiority in exchange.

So the narcissist is making do with dominance instead of recognition. The lack of true recognition is like a chronic wound that requires constant bandaging. Scarily, the narcissist bandages their own despair and terror of going unrecognized by further exerting dominance over the other person. They require a constant supply of feeling dominant, or they will psychologically implode. The narcissist, then, is dependent on the other. They need the other's submission to keep feeling powerful. In a sense—despite how self-assured and independent they may seem—the narcissist cannot exist alone. They need someone else to dominate to feel like they exist.

Your Happiness Threatens the Narcissist's Dominance

Feeling vitalized while in a relationship with a narcissist punctures their dominance. Showing your independent existence and vitality through happiness creates a pull for the narcissist to recognize you. Doing so comes at the cost of them feeling dominant. How can a self-perceived king or queen show respect to a pauper? If that pauper seems content instead of obedient, the narcissist will not stand for it.

Who the Narcissist Chooses to Dominate

Narcissists can only dominate people who are vulnerable to them. Tragically, this means that children like Joe are the most common targets. They learn that their happiness makes their parent unhappy.

The narcissist's child must police themselves to not show any enthusiasm unless it reflects directly upon their parent. Joe's mother insisted on this. He could joke around with her, but not others. He had to restrict his friendships because she would make up reasons to ground him if he seemed excited about his social life.

It is painful to think about how the victims of such abuse have to dislocate themselves from themselves just to stay out of danger. They cannot have spontaneous experiences of joy. They cannot even know how they feel, because that involves looking inward instead of outward at the narcissist. All of these ways of being provide the narcissist with what they want: to know they have power and control over the victim.

3

The Pressure to Believe What the Narcissistic Parent Says

> *Was it impossible to defend yourself against your narcissistic parent's accusations?*
> *Did you find yourself believing that you were as bad as they claimed?*
> *Does it feel like it's just a matter of time before other people "discover" how bad you are?*

Many survivors of narcissistic parents wonder why they didn't just talk back to the parent. They may go over and over past scenes of abuse and blame themselves for letting the parent "get away with it." This train of thought may even lead the survivor to conclude that there is something about them that the narcissist picked up on, which led to the abuse. Someone else who was "stronger," their reasoning goes, probably would not have gone along with such abuse.

Such reactions are certainly understandable. However, these survivors do not take into full consideration all the ways in which a narcissistic parent can pressure a child into believing the destructive messages they send. In this chapter, I am going to explain a process that is often used by people with severe personality pathology to coerce others to go along with abuse. As you understand how your narcissistic parent may have used this tactic with you, my hope is that you find more compassion for yourself and what you were up against. At the end of this chapter, you may shift from blaming yourself for not "speaking up" more to considering that you did exactly what you had to do to survive an otherwise impossible situation.

The name of this process is pathological projective identification (PPI). It has a lot of syllables, but can be simply described. I will give an example of it at work and use that example to explain it more fully.

How Pathological Projective Identification (PPI) Works

As described in Chapter 1, a narcissist's top priority is always to keep their dreaded sense of worthlessness at bay. PPI allows them to do this—at the expense of the person they're doing it with. Let me explain.

> *Sarah was in her twenties when she came to therapy to recover from the effects of growing up with a narcissistic father. She recalled an incident that perfectly illustrates pathological projective identification.*
>
> *When Sarah was seven years old, her family went to a restaurant to celebrate her father's birthday. While they were all singing "Happy Birthday," she remembers staring at a sculpture at the front of the restaurant that had caught her eye. She was captivated by it.*

Her father's worthlessness was triggered when she didn't pay full attention to him during the birthday song. He must have believed she didn't think he was important enough for her to pay attention to. The resulting feelings of shame and inadequacy would have been too much for him to bear, so he likely denied these feelings to himself. Instead, he "saw" the shame and worthlessness as residing in Sarah. She was the inadequate one for letting her attention wander at such an important moment for him.

His anger toward her grew. The power he felt in his fury would have been preferable to the helplessness he felt in being unable to stop her from throwing his worthlessness in his face. He just needed her to justify his anger at her for being so "worthless." He looked sternly at her until he caught her eye, and she was immediately flushed with embarrassment. She knows what she did, he may have told himself.

After the song ended, he walked to where she was sitting at the table and asked her to go with him to the restaurant lobby. In contemptuous whispered tones, he told her that if she couldn't even pay attention to him on his birthday, then she could just stay home next time. He told her that he couldn't believe how selfish she was being. Tears welled up in her eyes and she pleaded with him, telling him how sorry she was. She loathed herself for having "made him" feel this way. Why am I such a bad daughter? she had painfully asked herself.

This is how a narcissistic parent can transfer their own feelings of worthlessness to their child. Sarah's father initially must have felt his own worthlessness when he attributed her wandering gaze to mean he was unimportant to her. Instead of taking responsibility for his own feelings, he engaged in a process of "finding" the worthless feeling in his "offending" daughter instead of himself. Then he influenced her to experience these feelings as her own. He did this by ragefully attacking her character.

He felt much more in control and protected from his feelings of worthlessness when he saw the pain she was in. His lack of empathy made this a good bargain for him. Her pain just did not matter compared to the pain he was spared by doing this to her. And this was mostly an unconscious process for him. This was something he regularly did to manage such threats to his fragile self-worth.

So, put more formally: Pathological projective identification involves a parent relocating an unbearable sense of themselves and "finding" it in their child (Seligman, 2018; Reid & Kealy, 2022). Next, the parent acts coercively to influence the child to see the relocated fragment of the parent's experience as the child's own. In essence, the parent influences the child to identify with the unwanted feelings that he or she is projecting. This is a fragile arrangement, however, and the parent must continually work to keep the location of the unwanted experience in the child rather than themselves.

Why PPI Works

The Need to Share a Reality with a Parent

It is essential for a child to know that they inhabit the same reality as their parent. When the parent is well-adjusted, this can form the basis of a healthy child-parent bond and the child's developing sense of self. When the parent is narcissistic, the child is put into a predicament. Now they have to psychologically contort themselves to fit into the narcissistic parent's distorted reality. The child does not have the option of insisting the narcissistic parent fit into their reality, as the narcissistic parent's agenda of self-promotion does not include meeting their child's developing needs.

In order to fit into and share in the narcissistic parent's reality, it is essential for the child to accept and identify with the parent's projections of their own unwanted feelings. Why? Because if the child does not do this their parent will not recognize them as part of their reality. This is a profoundly distressing experience for the child. It feels like being nobody to no one and is inherently traumatic. That is, such experience overwhelms the child's abilities to cope at the time. The child cannot go to a different adult who cares for them and restore their sense of being known by an important other person. Instead the child must find a way sacrifice their own perspective to stay known by the parent they have.

For example, let's say that Sarah had said to her father, "Dad, I think you're way off here. I love you and am happy to celebrate your birthday. The statue just caught my eye, but it absolutely did not mean that I don't think you're important. Why are you accusing me of this?"

He would most likely just have told her that she didn't know what she was talking about and that he was right. If Sarah stuck to her guns, she would be in an area where what she thought was flatly denied by her father. She would risk feeling psychologically and emotionally unknown to him. Children must avoid such experiences at all costs.

As the situation with Sarah actually played out, she immediately took in her father's projection of his own worthlessness and identified herself as the worthless one so that he didn't have to—again, all unconsciously. In doing so, she spared herself from feeling disowned by him.

The Parent's Certainty

The narcissistic parent is absolute in their insistence that their perceptions are correct. In a deep-seated way, Sarah's father's claim that she did not think he was important enough to pay attention to was not up for debate. He concretely saw her as the person who had made him feel worthless, and now she was going to pay for it.

Children on the receiving end of a narcissistic parent's projections cannot effectively defend themselves to the parent. The parent already knows what the child has done. This certainty reflects the parent's psychological disturbance.

Someone who is not narcissistic might feel wounded seeing their daughter turn her attention elsewhere during the birthday song, too. The difference is that this non-narcissistic parent wouldn't presume to know that their daughter was thinking. The non-narcissistic parent might ask their daughter what had caught her eye and be able to hear and believe her when she explained that she couldn't stop looking at the sculpture because of its color.

In such exchanges with a good-enough parent, there is still room for collaboration and dialogue, even when strong feelings are stirred up in the parent. How confusing for a child to see their parent—whom they are biologically programmed to look up to—be so certain and so wrong at the same time. This confusion is usually resolved by the child deciding they are wrong and the parent is right, no matter what their own judgment tells them.

Scapegoat survivors of narcissistic parents who have experienced this kind of pathological projective identification can have difficulty knowing what they really think for themselves. They have had to abandon their own judgment many times to go along with the parent's pathological certainty. It is usually not until survivors are working to recover from this abuse that they get to know and trust their own perspective again.

The Parent's Intrusiveness

Pathological projective identification sends a call to the child that has to be answered. The child feels the weight of the parent's desperation behind this tactic. The child's dependence on the parent sharpens their sensitivity to the parent's psychological demands and motivation to meet them. The very nature of projective identification involves one person needing an unbearable state of mind to exist in someone else. Without this, a profound breakdown could occur.

The child feels an imperative to orient to and comply with what the parent is looking to find in them. When pathological projective identification is at play, the parent will always find what he is looking for—and the child will help him do so. The child assists in this process by heeding the call to be what the parent requires him to be.

Sarah experienced this pressure to attend to her father's projections as fear of what he would do to her if she did not. At first, she could not exactly name what she feared he might do. Over time, we grew to understand that she felt like something terrible would happen if she did not play along with how he seemed to have to see her. Therapy helped her understand that the "something terrible" might be the psychological collapse of her relationship with her father and potentially her ability to remain intact if she did not identify with his projection.

The Need to Identify with the Parent's Unwanted Feelings

For a child caught in this arrangement with a parent, one of the most insidious aspects is how terrible the alternative of not identifying with the parent's projections would be. A child looks to his parent for accurate reinforcement of who he is in the world. A parent's contingent and affirming responsiveness to the child's expressions lead to such reinforcement (Seligman, 2018).

A lot happens in these arrangements. The parent is saying "I am here and exist independently from you, and you are there and exist independently from me. I am curious about you and want to understand as much about you as you will allow me." The child now has the requisite space and relational context needed to develop a sense of their authentic way of being with themselves and with others.

In pathological projective identification, no such space exists between the parent and child. The parent is saying, "I am here and terrified. No, wait, the problem is over there in you. You are terrible. Why are you so terrible?" The parent cannot regard the child as an independent other person to be found out about. Instead, the parent already knows who the child is—the receptacle of their projection—yet also has no clue. The child feels this. He can either be known in a pseudo way as what his parent is coercing him to identify, with or he can feel completely unknown—and unknowable—to the parent.

To feel unknown by and unknowable to a primary caregiver can mean that one does not really exist, and that the parent does not really exist. Such encounters yield a sense of unendurable emptiness, void, terror, despair, and rage. As crushing and ill-fitting as it may feel to identify with the parent's projections, the alternative is likely worse.

4

The Narcissistic Parent's Rage

> *Was your parent prone to explosive bouts of rage?*
> *Did they justify their rage by claiming they were the victim?*
> *Did your parent refuse to be accountable for what they said or did while raging?*

If any of these three questions apply to your experience then you may be very familiar with narcissistic rage. A narcissist's rage can feel—and sometimes be—life-threatening to the recipient. In this chapter, narcissistic rage will be defined and illustrated. Its impacts on the scapegoat child will be examined. The most important thing for survivors is to identify, value, and respect the ways they survived such rage—especially when survival required submission to the narcissistic parent.

What Is Narcissistic Rage?

When a narcissistic parent explodes in rage at their child, they seek to destroy first and ask questions later. Children who have suffered such bouts of narcissistic rage often describe feeling hated by the parent—and for good reason. The narcissist does in fact hate the object of their rage while in this state. They may even convey a sense of murderousness toward the "offender."

Children who have survived such parenting speak of the spine-chilling turns that would happen when their parents grew angry. Mom or Dad seemed possessed by a demon—there was something in and behind their eyes that terrified the child. Survivors knew that there was no pleading or arguing to assuage the parent's rage once this turn occurred. The only way to respond—and survive—was to submissively freeze until it was over. Showing fear and accepting blame for the narcissist's rage and hatred was the only hope the child had to survive it.

> *During Perry's whole childhood, his father would explode into screaming tirades at his mother. Perry described him as being suspicious and derisive toward her, particularly during their nightly dinners. His father would perceive an offense from Perry's mother and slam his hands down on the table. He would tell her things like "You are so stupid! How could you even ask that question?!" or "Just shut up, you don't know what the hell you're talking about."*
>
> *Perry's father would then ratchet up and up to find more reasons why his wife deserved his criticism and hatred in that moment. She would endure these bouts of rage until he decided he had finished with her. Perry knew that when his father was raging, the worst thing he could do would be to talk back or walk away. He—and his mother—just had to sit there while his father let loose on her. Freezing in this manner was a very adaptive move on Perry's part, as it minimized the damage inflicted by his father.*

Why Does a Narcissistic Parent Get Enraged?

I find it useful to think of the narcissist's psychology when trying to understand their rage reactions. As described in Chapter 2, the narcissist feels a core sense of worthlessness and copes by disowning those feelings and consciously insisting on their specialness, importance, and superiority while coercing others to treat them in kind. This coping mechanism is largely unconscious and requires low empathy and remorselessness, two deficits most narcissists come by easily.

When this type of fragilely assembled psychology comes into contact with the slightest failure of another to reflect back the narcissist's artificially inflated sense of self, they may leverage rage to teach that person a lesson about how they should be treated. Any experience where the narcissist feels hindered in their ability to see themselves—and/or have others treat them—as superior can set off their rage.

A narcissistic mother, for example, may see herself as so supremely caring that her children should show only gratitude and deference toward her. Trouble ensues when her son protests that he wants to play with his friends instead of stay home to pick up his room. In her mind, anything but obedience to her wishes means that her son thinks she is worthless. In this moment, she has to relocate—via pathological projective identification—that sense of worthlessness to her son rather than herself. Rage is very handy for this. By exploding into a screaming, scathing assessment of him for being "selfish, disrespectful, inconsiderate, and impossible," she gets to see him as the worthless one instead of herself. Her child will also tend to believe her, because her authority as his mother makes him assume she knows him best. He may also de-escalate her rage by accepting her accusations as true.

Thus, narcissistic rage can serve to restore the narcissist's fragile inner equilibrium and serve as a warning to their children. A narcissistic parent who demonstrates a willingness to make their children the focus of rage lets the kids know the dire consequences of not complying with the parent's expectations. In short, their rage is the threat the child must now remain wary of and seek to minimize. It is not just that the narcissistic parent expects special treatment from their children—they often threaten to make the child feel hated and worthless if they do not comply.

One of the cruelest aspects of a narcissistic parent's anger is the calculated way they employ it. In most cases, narcissistic parents know to keep their rages hidden from disapproving others outside the family. They know when they can explode in rage and when they cannot. Survivors of this treatment learn to expect rage behind closed doors—not in public.

> *John would get yelled at almost every day by his narcissistic mother for various "offenses." He vividly recalled her screaming at the top of her lungs at him, then the phone ringing. She would pick up, midtirade, and sweetly say, "Oh, hiiiii, I am so glad you called. I was just thinking of you . . ." At the time, he couldn't highlight her obvious hypocrisy, because that would have only enraged her further. Later in therapy, he was able to helpfully see how his mother's deceptiveness reflected her pathological narcissism.*

Can the Child Avoid the Narcissistic Parent's Rage?

The writing above may imply that a child can avoid a narcissist's rage so long as they reflect back the narcissist's inflated self-worth. Survivors of such parents know different. Sometimes, it is a child's mere existence—not what the child does or does not do—that evokes the parent's sense of worthlessness. When a narcissistic parent sees qualities in their child that they covet, they seek to punish that child. The narcissistic parent's motto is something like, "If you cannot join 'em, beat 'em,"—much to the child's detriment.

The unfortunate reality for such a child is that she will have to endure bout after bout of the parent's narcissistic rage and hatred. She may be smarter, kinder, more genuine, stronger—whatever it is that makes the narcissistic parent feel inadequate. Not unlike the stepmother in the fairy tale Snow White, a narcissistic parent looks at their child and realizes they are no longer the "fairest in the land," and this enrages them. They do not need to ask a huntsman to take the child into the woods and bring back her heart. Instead, the narcissistic parent leverages their authority and the other family members'[2] fear of reprisal to blame and devalue the child until the parent once again feels convinced of their superiority.

---

[2] I refer to a specific type of family structure a lot. This includes the narcissistic parent, their enabler partner and other children along with the scapegoat child. These dynamics can occur in a lot of other family organizations. A single-parent household, for example, with a narcissistic parent can also result in scapegoating a child.

The Impact of Narcissistic Rage on the Child

Learning to Freeze and Submit to Survive

In the literature on attachment trauma, there are four basic ways to respond to a threat (Walker, 2013). The list below categorizes the appropriateness of each response Appropriateness is measured by the odds of victory if directly confronting the threat and on how permanent the threat is to the person. For example, someone encountering an aggressive stray dog has low odds of victory and low permanence. This person could appropriately flee, freeze, or try to submit to the threat.

The Four Responses to Trauma

1. **Fight**: Summon anger and aggression to seek and destroy the threat. (Odds of victory = high, permanence of threat = low.)
2. **Flee**: Leverage adrenaline to create a safe distance between you and threat. (Odds of victory = low, permanence of threat = low.)
3. **Freeze**: Use fear to stay very still until the threat has passed. (Odds of victory = low, permanence of threat = low.)
4. **Submit**: Curry favor with the threat and get them to take mercy on you. (Odds of victory = low, permanence of threat = high.)

The 4 Responses to Traumatic Threat

A chart with "Odds of Victory" on the y-axis (Low to High) and "Permanence of Threat" on the x-axis (Low to High), showing: **fight** (High odds, Low permanence), **flee** (Low odds, Low permanence), **freeze** (middle), **submit** (Low odds, High permanence).

A child faced with a raging parent has very low odds of victory and very high permanence of threat. Thus, the child's appropriate options are to freeze or submit. These responses both communicate the implicit message that the narcissist is in charge. Given that the source of the narcissist's rage is the feeling that someone—often the child—is not reflecting back their superiority, these modes of response help the narcissist restore their inflated sense of self-worth. To fight or flee the narcissist would only further enrage them.

So, for the moment, the tragic reality of the child is having to freeze and/or submit when the narcissistic parent flies into a rage at him or her. This often does not come naturally, as most children are born with a source of vitality and energy that must be curtailed to respond in this way. This is where self-diminishing beliefs come in.

How Shame and Self-Loathing Can Be Adaptive

One of the very adaptive ways one can ready oneself to freeze in fear and/or offer a submissive countenance is to develop beliefs about oneself that engender such reactions. Janina Fisher, an expert in understanding and coping with the effects of prolonged abusive childhoods, has described how self-diminishing beliefs can make it easier to submit and/or freeze (Fisher, 2017). A child who believes he is defective will have a much easier time doing whatever his narcissistic parent tells him to do than a child who believes he deserves to be treated with respect. Thus, he is spared from further rage attacks and more likely to survive his childhood.

Here I want to mention another challenge to appreciating the ways in which you have survived: feeling traumatically triggered. When a survivor has to invoke the freeze or submit response toward a raging narcissistic parent, he likely feels small, weak, and endangered. Once that child grows up to be an adult, sometimes a thought, cue in the environment, or word said by another can catapult him back to being that same submitting child who knew what strategies he needed to survive. In these moments, the adult does not feel like the adult he is but rather the child he was.

Richard Schwartz uses the term "blending" to describe such moments (Schwartz & Sweezy, 2019). The traumatized part of the survivor is evoked and takes over the adult's sense of himself. When this happens, it can reinforce to the adult survivor that he actually is the way he feels in such triggered states. Such experiences are the legacy of surviving narcissistic rage and are dealt with by cultivating connection to the present reality. When in such a triggered state, the survivor can use his awareness of his adult self to attend to the part of him that feels afraid and work to soothe this part. This, in short, is an exercise in deep mindfulness.

5

Why a Narcissist Plays Nice in Public and Abuses in Private

> *Did you have a narcissistic parent who showered people outside the home with deference, respect and charm? Did that same parent have no trouble turning against you once the doors to the outside world closed? Did you constantly have to worry about your narcissistic parent feeling embarrassed by your behavior out in public such that you would hear about it later?*

If you've experienced your narcissistic parent as having two faces—one for you, where seemingly anything would go, and one for the outside world, where they acted like a people pleaser to others—this chapter is for you. There is a good reason why a narcissistic parent has no trouble acting abusively toward those closest to them while exalting those farther away. In this chapter, I explain why this often happens and offer some case examples. Next, I explain how this can lead to the belief that your opinion of others is far less important than their opinions of you.

A narcissistic person is constantly ranking people they meet according to their perceived status because they want to know where they stand in relation to everyone else. Typically when a narcissist is around people they perceive to be of higher status, they feel special being in the company of someone so "grand." They often have difficulty seeing others as being of equal status to them. However, as many scapegoat children can attest, they perceive those closest them to be of lower status.

This constant slotting of people as being either above or below the narcissist is a fragile arrangement and can leave them feeling weak in their core selves. This experience, which many narcissists would ardently deny, can lead them to only see people who are farther away as higher status, while those of lower status tend to be closer to them. The narcissistic person can feel very vulnerable to being shamed or humiliated by someone of higher status, but holds no such fear toward someone they regard as lower status.

This is why the narcissistic head of a family may show a lot of respect and deference toward people of authority outside the family while having no problem being emotionally abusive and neglectful toward members of the family. The external authority poses the threat of rejecting the narcissistic parent, which would be intolerable for that parent. However, as the child is dependent on the narcissistic parent, they pose no such risk of humiliating rejection.

> *Mike was in therapy after surviving a narcissistic mother. He recalled how she used to act exceedingly charming toward anyone she encountered outside of the home. Teachers, other parents, even his friends would see a mother who was interested in what they had to say, laughed at their jokes, and constantly asked them questions about themselves. But when he was home alone with her, she would walk around*

> *the house and find excuses to yell at him. She would claim he'd failed to do a chore she had asked him to do and launch into a screaming tirade at him for being selfish and taking her for granted. Mike recalled that if the doorbell rang while she was screaming at him, she would instantly change her demeanor and present the smiling façade she offered to the outside world.*
>
> *Mike was struck by how seamlessly his mother could move from acting tyrannically toward him to cowering in the face of those outside the home. She seemed to fear their opinion of her far more than she worried about Mike's. Unfortunately, to have her regard him as lower status than so many others in her life damaged Mike's own sense of self-worth. He understandably adopted the belief that his opinion of others was less important than their opinion of him.*

Tiffany was another scapegoat survivor of a narcissistic father who managed his own feelings of being lower status by transferring them to her.

> *Tiffany recalled how he would want to drive around their hometown and look at houses that were extremely expensive. He would then tell her that the people who owned those houses had great lives and were really important. Typically when they got home, he would find a reason to yell at her in ways that left her feeling like he was irreparably disappointed in who she was as a person. Tiffany's father saw the people in the big homes as being higher status than him, yet had no trouble treating Tiffany as though she were lower status than him.*

Both Tiffany and Mike's experiences led them to believe that they were of lower status than others. Such beliefs are common for scapegoat survivors of narcissistic abuse. It can be hard not to assess your status in comparison to others when you've been treated this way. Doing so was a matter of survival while the abuse was happening, and adopting the belief that you are lower status than others actually requires a consistent assessment of status.

6

The Altruistic Narcissist

> *Did your narcissistic parent seem like everyone else's best friend?*
> *Did this parent go out of their way to help others while expecting constant gratitude?*
> *Were you wary of accepting this parent's help because they would later accuse you of being ungrateful and selfish?*

Narcissism comes in many forms. The one common denominator is that those around the narcissist either feel "less-than" or face harsh repudiation. I want to focus on the altruistic narcissist, because their cloak of kindness can confuse their victims. Such narcissists go way out of their way to curate the image of a selfless caregiver. This image is insincere, there to combat an inner sense of worthlessness rather than reflecting genuine care for and protection of others.

In this chapter, I will explain how narcissists can use surface-level altruism as an antidote to their core sense of worthlessness. This false altruism requires tremendous inward self-absorption and self-promotion, features that do not align with the concept of altruism. As a result, such narcissists must work extra hard to "see" their hyper self-focus (or "selfishness") in others rather than themselves. I will then describe the signs of an altruistic narcissist, followed by a case description of a client's narcissistic mother who used him as a prop for her altruistic act.

Using "Altruism" for the Narcissist's Purposes

Some narcissists are pretty transparent in their grandiosity. Others are less so. Altruistic narcissists view themselves as supreme caregivers. They base their inflated self-concept on this supposed ability, then expect others to react to them as though they are the caring, generous people they want to seem like. As a result, it can sometimes take a little longer to identify this kind of narcissist.

Parenthood can seem very appealing to the altruistic narcissist. They get to demonstrate their—supposedly—superior caregiving abilities to a child, whom they may assume will be nothing but appreciative. What a rude awakening when the baby comes into this world as a bundle of joy—and needs! Children require a caretaker who is ready to give a lot more than they receive. That is not what the child of an altruistic narcissist gets.

The altruistic narcissist can maintain their fragile self-esteem so long as their grandiose sense of self—and entitlement to others' reflections of that self—go uninterrupted. Their primary occupation in life is maintaining this perception of themselves. They are incapable of experiencing lasting and sincere loving feelings toward another person. As appealing as parenthood may seem, the reality of a child looking up at them with the expectation of being met with genuine love and affection can actually feel terrible for this type of parent. The altruistic narcissist is faced with the fact that they do not really want to provide care to their own child. Their identity as a nurturer is a sham; their inability to feel love for their child proves it. If they admitted this to themselves, their inflated self-concept would crumble and they would be left with their dreaded worthlessness.

On top of this unflattering realization about their lack of genuine care for others, parenthood poses constant interruptions to the altruistic narcissist's antidotal grandiosity and entitlement. Such interruptions can lead to the parent feeling their dreaded worthlessness. A child's rightful and persistent needs for care, feeding, attention, and love are about the child—not the parent. For most parents, this is not a problem. For a narcissistic parent, the volume and intensity of the child's needs require them to interrupt their focus on themselves. Unless they can feel appreciated by the baby or others witnessing how "well" they are parenting, the narcissistic parent will see little motivation to offer care. Doing so does not reinforce their inflated sense of being a caregiver because they cannot get their child to comply with it.

My nine years working with scapegoat clients has taught me that survivors believe that in order to receive care from another, they must find a way to make it in that person's own interest. They can expect care so long as it benefits the other person. They may feel a mandate to show immense gratitude or flattery at acts of kindness toward them. These feelings were come by honestly, because that is exactly what their narcissistic parent required from them. Therapy often allows these survivors to see this pattern as a reflection of their ability to adapt to and survive a very awful and one-sided relationship.

> *Sarah's mother worked as a psychologist, and Sarah knew she saw herself as a nurturing woman. In one of her sessions, Sarah recalled her mother flying into rages whenever she left any toys out as a young child. As she grew, her mother reacted to her as though all of her needs were "too much." She insisted that Sarah always watch herself, lest she take limited attention away from "those who needed it"—like her younger brother. In one of the most searingly painful moments of Sarah's childhood, she asked for her mother's attention, wanting to show her a drawing she had made. Her mother pulled her aside and contemptuously said, "You know Sarah, the world does not revolve around you!"*

Sarah's mother is a good example of an altruistic narcissist. She curated an image as maternal provider, yet consistently met her daughter's real needs with contempt, exasperation, and blame.

Why the Altruistic Narcissist Must Hide Their Selfishness

All of the narcissist's efforts to prop themselves up are to stave off their core feeling of worthlessness. To do this, the altruistic narcissist needs to seem like a selfless provider to others. However, their strategies of inflating their sense of importance and expecting others to comply are inherently self-absorbed. The altruistic narcissist must fiercely deny this fact, as it could unravel what is staving off their worthlessness.

The narcissist denies her own self-absorption by unconsciously relocating this quality in others and reacting to them as though they are the selfish ones. This relocation is best done in relationships where she has authority. As such, a child offers a convenient target. The child's existence and expectation of love reminds the narcissistic parent of how little she can care about anyone but herself. In order to combat this reminder, she will work to see her child as defective to excuse her inability to love him.

Part of this accused defectiveness may include perceiving and reacting to him as though he is the selfish one. When a kid is told by his mother that asking for a piece of candy means that all he cares about is himself and he is incredibly selfish, he tends to believe her. In this case, the narcissistic mother can readily claim that she remains selfless and altruistic but had the rotten luck of giving birth to the world's most selfish child. Quite a ruse, but not an uncommon one in households with a narcissistic parent.

Four Signs of an Altruistic Narcissist

Very Low Patience

When an altruistic narcissist "gives" something to another person, they are doing it solely to get a reflection of their grandiose, caring self. If the other person requires more than a brief symbolic gesture, the narcissist may quickly grow impatient and show frustration with the recipient.

> *John had an altruistically narcissistic mother. She would scream at and berate him when he "misbehaved" (which seemed to be three times a day at least), then act as if she had done nothing wrong. One night, after yelling at him for not taking the trash out, she came into his room and, in stark contrast to her previous tone, sweetly said she could take him to school the next day. In the morning, John ran a few minutes late, and the entire car ride was filled with her berating him, saying his inconsiderateness and selfishness had made her late for work.*

Children of altruistic narcissists, like John, learn to make it easy for others to care for them. They intuitively know their parents don't have much in the tank for them, and that it's best not to test their willingness to show care.

Constant Expectation of Gratitude

An altruistic narcissist not only expects to have to expend very little real effort to help others, but also requires displays of gratitude.

> *John hated opening presents on Christmas mornings. He had to train himself to show wide-eyed surprise, delight, and demonstrations of appreciation whenever he opened a gift from his mother. He knew that if he didn't do that and walk across the room to hug her, she would grow angry and abusive toward him.*

Altruistic narcissists will vary in how explicitly they convey this expectation. If they have power or authority over someone, they may brazenly show that they expect gratitude—insisting that the other says thank you right away, for instance. If they are not in a position of power and the other person does not meet their standard of gratitude, the narcissist may just seethe and speak ill of that person when they can.

The Desire to Enforce Rules

Rules are a means to an end for the altruistic narcissist. They find ways to be on the side of enforcing them and take satisfaction in catching and punishing the rule breakers. It gives them an opportunity to see someone else as worthless and deserving of punishment. As discussed above, seeing others as worthless offers an antidotal relief from their own sense of worthlessness.

> *John's mother would set up rules that centered around him doing certain chores around the house. Every time she screamed and verbally abused him, it was based on the premise that he had broken one of these rules. She felt justified in her treatment of him because he was so "defiant" and "disobedient." To John, she seemed to sadistically enjoy catching him breaking these rules and the ensuing punishments she then got to administer.*

"Lost Cause" Friends and Partners

A lot of times, an altruistic narcissist will presume to know what is best for a friend or partner. The narcissist will then target this person as someone who needs fixing. She may talk about this person as though they are a lost cause who just cannot seem to make the right choices. The altruistic narcissist may grow frustrated and angry with this person for not following her advice and prescriptions. By being close to such people, the narcissist can cast them as the defective ones in the relationship.

Illustration of an Altruistic Narcissist

Nancy was born to two alcoholic parents. Her mother was concerned with appearances in public and modeled chronic, deceitful, and mean-spirited behavior in private. Her father was an accomplished soldier but recused himself from taking an active role in the family. Nancy herself identified with her mother's contemptuous attitude toward her brother and father.

The attention her parents paid her was as a trophy: they would bring her and her brother out to their drunken parties and show off how "well-behaved" their kids were. Nancy would repeatedly try to be the adult and admonish her parents for drinking. She learned that she did not really matter in this world beyond the purposes she could serve for others. She hated this predicament to her core and could not stand how worthless she felt.

From an early age, she carried a reservoir of rage that she would find opportunities to release when she could get away with it. On the one hand, she had to act like a well-behaved, caring young woman, but on the other, she wanted to make others pay for how excruciating life felt for her. Thus began her life of profound self-deception— acting saintly on the surface while privately exacting her vengeance on those vulnerable to her.

Nancy adorned herself with the trappings of altruism to keep her rage at bay. She studied education in college and became a teacher for children labeled as "socially and emotionally disturbed." Teaching a group of students who were already marginalized by the school system afforded her extra cover when she was overly punitive with a pupil. She would typically identify one male student in her class as a "behavior problem"—usually the most strong-willed of the group. She could then blame her cold and punitive treatment on the student.

"I am trying to be a good teacher, but I just cannot get through a lesson without _____ acting up." Such statements to her colleagues served as justification for her hateful and sharp ways of speaking to the student. She would also devise special ways to antagonize him so that she could have an excuse to take her rage out on him. Creating an arbitrary reason he could not go to recess—announced the minute all the kids were headed out the door—was one of her favorite tactics. The boy would often cry out in exasperated fury, which would justify her holding him back in the classroom and terrorizing him with threats of expulsion or suspension for the duration of the recess.

Nancy married a man who was very pliable and deferential toward her. When she gave birth to her first child—a son—she assumed imperious authority over how he should be raised. Her husband readily stood aside or colluded with her when she blamed her son for her inability to love him. She curated an image among her friends as a doting mother. Once she was alone with her son, however, she had no patience for him.

Most parents experience an internal wealth of love from which to meet their child's needs and demands. It gives them meaning and joy to do so. Nancy, in contrast, did not have this wealth to rely upon. She would muster energy to care for her son if others were around, but behind closed doors, she quickly grew weary of him. If he called to her in such moments, she would exclaim, "What?!" Her tone carried a combination of threat and exasperation.

It was unbearable to know that when she saw what made most people fill with love and joy—say, her son playing with blocks—she felt nothing. Worse than nothing: she would grow angry at him for reminding her of how vacant she was. In such moments, she preferred to be filled with rage. Her anger could be directed away from herself and toward the boy. Maybe he wasn't obeying her instructions. That's why he deserved her wrath. There was nothing wrong with her for feeling nothing for her child. If he were less rotten, she would certainly be filled with the motherly love she must possess . . . right?

She found that she could only feel like the good mother she wanted to be when being watched by others. So, she made sure to get out into public as often as possible with her son. Just as her own parents had paraded her around in front of their friends, she paraded her son to reinforce her wishful assertion that she was good on the inside.

For Nancy, everyone in her life became a bit player with the sole function of hiding how empty and cruel she felt. It seemed that as long as she could secretively target someone as the source of her inability to love, she could function well in the world.

She rotated through friends. Initially she would see them as wayward souls she could point in the right direction. As the friendship progressed they would reveal signs of self-worth and empowerment. Nancy could not tolerate such displays because they did not seem as dependent on her. She would secretly seethe inside at their "selfishness", discard them, and find a new lost cause to befriend.

She gave birth to a daughter three years after her son. This child was much closer in character to Nancy, and did not stand up to her the way her son often would. Her daughter was a much more willing to go along with her efforts to blame someone else for her cruel intentions.

As her son grew and increasingly became the target for her rage, she would often act proportionately kind to her daughter. It was as if she blamed her internal bitterness on her son and used her daughter to promote the wished-for truth that she could be sincerely kind and good. However, it was all an act, and she knew it. She had to divorce her husband after fourteen years of marriage because he had grown weary of her fits of rage and left her for another woman. She received full custody, and this gave her free rein to continue splitting up her children psychologically with impunity.

Nancy died from brain cancer ate age 50. Her son had taken to caring for her as she met her end. At one point while he was helping carry her back to bed, she said, "You've always been my true strength." This statement made no sense to him at the time. He had always thought of himself as a bad person. Why else would she have treated him so wickedly? Years later, in therapy, he grew to understand that she was crediting him with bearing the truth she could not. He knew firsthand how little genuine care, love, or empathy she could hold toward him—or anybody. And he bore all that she saddled him with and did not break. For someone whose psychological life depended on a lie, having a son she could hate instead of herself really did mean he was "her true strength."

At Nancy's funeral service, the pastor and attendees kept saying that she was everyone's best friend. Everyone extolled the virtues she'd worked so hard to curate: her care for those less fortunate, her willingness to listen to others, and her nurturing ways. Even the son who knew the other side of her joined this chorus. He gave a eulogy that portrayed her as she insisted on being seen—at the time it was not psychologically safe enough for him to speak the truth of his experience. Years later, as her influence waned, he would gain clarity on who his mother actually was, and how he had never been the horrible things she claimed he was.

This illustration highlights the duplicity of the altruistic narcissist. The scapegoat survivor of such a parent may feel confused at the disparity between the what happens in the home versus what the public sees from this parent. Survivors may encounter invalidation when they attempt to say what things were really like growing up. The purpose of this illustration is to offer an example that validates how things were not as they seemed with an altruistic narcissist.

7

The Enabler Parent

"The only thing necessary for the triumph of evil is for good men to do nothing."
–Edmund Burke

> *Did your other parent adopt a "see no evil, hear no evil" approach to your suffering?*
> *Did this parent seem emotionally uninvolved with you?*
> *Did you feel a pressure to act like everything was fine around this parent?*

Good things do not survive in the world unless they are protected. Think of a human baby. As cute, fun, and loving as they are, they are equally vulnerable. Most often, these awesome creatures receive joy, warmth, and protection by their caretakers. In the natural order, the young and defenseless are to be loved and protected by the older and stronger.

Sometimes, tragically, something unnatural happens. A child is born to someone motivated by something other than human connection. This person wants to see others—even their own children—suffer. They prize the feeling of power and control they get from controlling and dominating another human being. This feeling becomes so valued that no appeal to morality will impede them.

In my practice, most of my clients come from families with one narcissistically abusive parent. As they were growing up, the other "enabler" parent was typically less overtly abusive, but passive and compliant in the face of the other parent's abuse. This enabler parent buried themselves in work, alcohol, extramarital affairs, and/or household tasks in order to avoid intervening in what was happening to their children under their roof.

This chapter will discuss surviving and recovering from going unprotected from narcissistic abuse by the enabler parent. When a child is chronically derided, blamed, and devalued without intervention by the enabler parent, it is tragically easy for that child to conclude that they do not deserve protection. They may even conclude that they deserve to be abused and neglected.

What the Enabler's Underprotection Looks Like

In my experience, a narcissist does not get away with hurting his or her children without the endorsement, implicit or otherwise, of the other parent. I suspect that many narcissists choose partners who are meek and submissive so that they will not encounter resistance. They may search for partners with whom they feel dominant.

The prevailing theme in the relationship becomes whether the narcissist will be made happy. The enabler partner makes that their life goal. They also know it is a fickle achievement. Despite their efforts, they can still be found inadequate in making the narcissist happy. This lack of consistency is designed to keep the partner feeling insecure about their worth in the narcissist's eyes. Enabler partners are usually unable—or unwilling—to recognize how they are being strategically tormented. Instead they double down on their efforts to please.

Once this type of pseudo-relationship is established, the fate of any resulting children is often sealed. The narcissistic parent will inevitably find fault with, devalue, and demean a child. The enabler parent only sees that the narcissist is unhappy and will want to make them happy. If the narcissist identifies the child as the reason for their unhappiness, the other parent will too. The enabler parent may join the narcissist in "ganging up" on the child. They may seem distracted or uninvolved while the narcissist abuses the child, perhaps finding a reason to be out of the house—work obligations, extramarital affairs, etc. Whatever the tactic, the enabler parent signals to the child that they will not be offering protection. Gallingly, the other parent communicates "better you than me" to the child getting abused. This attitude flies in the face of the concept of parenting, yet is unfortunately common in families ruled by narcissists.

> *Tom had a narcissistic mother and an enabler father. When he was four years old, he came out to say good night to both parents. His mother may have found him to be in too high of spirits and decided he needed to be knocked down. She asked him if he had brushed his teeth, and he told her he had. She recoiled with an overdramatic gasp and said, "Oh Tom, how can you tell a lie like that?"*

> *He had, in fact, brushed his teeth, so he was confused, but knew something bad was going to happen. He insisted that he had brushed them and was met with her turning to his father and saying, "Can you believe that he is standing there lying to us?" Tom's father put down his beer, grabbed Tom by the elbow, spun him around, and spanked him three times. To Tom, it was not the physical pain that was significant. The knowledge that he had a mother who wanted to set him up for such abuse—and a father who would go along with it—was.*
>
> *Tom's parents had very little love between them. A master-slave relationship does not afford such experience. They did find consensus when targeting Tom for trumped-up reasons. In therapy, Tom grew to suspect that his father addressed the lack of power in his marriage by joining his wife in feeling powerful against his son.*

Tom's father enabled his mother's mistreatment of Tom by taking her claims against Tom as the gospel. His father never contemplated challenging his wife's perspective. Empathy for his son's feelings did not deter him from doing her bidding. The enabler parent acts as though the destructive impact of the narcissistic parent's behavior on the child does not matter.

> *Jason grew up with a narcissistic mother and enabler father. His mother would ask Jason to perform chores, then scream at him for "not doing them right." His father divorced his mother when Jason was twelve. In his therapy, Jason initially said he was grateful that his father stayed local after the*

divorce. "My dad could have moved back home to California where he grew up."

When I asked Jason whether he could appeal to his father about how his mother was mistreating him, he said, "He would tell me that he knew she could be this way. He'd just tell me to try not to make her upset." No calls to Child Protective Services. No battle for custody of Jason and his siblings. In essence, Jason was told to appease his mother and suffer her abuse on his own.

Jason was told in no uncertain terms that he would not receive protection from his father. Since his father was his most viable parent, he had to find a way to continue thinking highly of him. At the start of therapy, Jason revealed he did this by forcing himself to believe that he did not deserve to be protected from his mother's abuse. Saying he was grateful that his father had stayed local after the divorce reflected this. Only if he believed he was undeserving of protection could this gesture seem like a show of parental love.

As an adult, Jason found new relationships inside and outside of therapy that afforded him the safety he had always sought. These new connections allowed him to identify and question the belief that he could not have asked anything more of his father. He grew to feel entitled to feeling safe in relationships and recognized how his father's passivity in the face of his mother's abuse had denied him this.

The Enabler's Psychology

Enabler parents were often forgotten children in their families of origin. They may have adapted to a "children should be seen and not heard" ethos. Typically, the enabler parent was not singled out and attacked as a child, but neither did they receive much attention or recognition from their parents.

When a child is ignored in this way, a deficit of needed self-esteem, empathy for self and others, and initiative can develop. Such people emerge from their childhoods believing that they are expendable and would be lucky to find a romantic partner who accepts them. They learned in their families of origin that they did not deserve consistent respect and connection, a belief that then guides their search for a romantic partner. They will often comply with this belief and find a partner who also ignores their needs in favor of his or her own.

When an enabler-to-be is met with romantic affection, they may be astounded. They may never have thought they would get such treatment. After a long history of deprivation, such affection will often be clung to regardless of the offerer's other traits.

A narcissist will see such a person as a preferable and relatively easy target. She seeks to find a partner she can control and manipulate with her affection, someone who is more interested in making the narcissist happy than making themselves happy. People who were chronically ignored by their parents were often so starved for affection that they will fit this bill.

Tom's father was an officer in the Army. He attended West Point, then served a tour in Vietnam. He was smitten with his eventual wife and did everything he could to win her affection, and her difficult moods only made him try harder to please her. She grew in hostility toward him as their wedding date approached, but he never considered walking away from the relationship.

In Tom's twelve years growing up with both of his parents in the house, he could only recall his mother screaming at his father—never the other way around. In the end, his father had a series of extramarital affairs that led to a divorce, effectively leaving Tom alone with his narcissistic mother.

Tom's father seems to not have had much of a center in himself. He was easily influenced and did not have empathy for Tom—just his wife and himself. Although Tom's father, unlike his wife, was not predisposed to active acts of cruelty, he had no trouble passively allowing her to commit them against his son. Tom's father's only goal in life was to find people who were happy with him. If these people showed disapproval toward someone other than him, he may have felt relief that he wasn't the one being rejected. He didn't have the innate instinct to protect those who were more vulnerable. As is unfortunately true of enabler parents, he didn't have the innate instinct to protect those who were more vulnerable.

8

The Scapegoat Child

> *Was it a matter of when, not if, you were blamed for something by your narcissistic parent?*
> *Did it seem impossible to deserve and get praise for who you were, not what you did?*
> *Did the rest of your family also see you as "the problem"?*

This chapter describes why certain children get selected as scapegoats, the impact of getting scapegoated, and how to use therapy to recover from this especially destructive form of abuse.

Sometimes a client comes into therapy telling horrific stories of the chronic and systematic abuse they have suffered. They recount how their caregivers criticized, humiliated, hurt, degraded and derided them at every opportunity. What makes this suffering most destructive is the abuser's conviction that it was what the child deserved. There is no sense of recrimination, accountability, or guilt for what they put the child through. Rather, there is an inscrutable self-righteousness in their cruel attitudes and behavior toward the victim. As you have read in previous chapters, there is also without fail a concerted effort to keep this abuse private from the world at large. The adult child recalls seeing the abusive caregiver charm people outside the home and keep their demonic cruelty behind closed doors—all the better to discredit the victim's credibility if they ever come forward to report the abuse. Welcome to the world of the narcissistic family's scapegoat.

Why a Narcissistic Family Scapegoats a Child

When a family is dominated by a narcissistic parent, a tremendous strain is put upon the family system. The narcissistic parent needs to feel superior to and in control over someone else. That makes anyone close to such a person a potential target. In a family system, the collective strain of the narcissist's need for a victim gets relieved when a single person is selected. The other members can breathe a sigh of relief, psychologically speaking, and join the narcissist in blaming the selected child for all the family's unhappiness.

If the narcissist has chosen their enabling spouse correctly or is a single parent they will enjoy unchecked authority in the family. Usually, a child cannot be scapegoated without the implicit permission of an enabler parent. The ringleader of abuse in the family requires that everyone see things as she sees them. If she sees the scapegoat as the abomination, then her partner and other children better agree with her. She uses any means necessary to coerce the enabler parent and the scapegoat's siblings into agreement. These other parties are enticed by having the favor of the narcissistic parent and deterred by the wrath that will follow if they dissent.

A narcissist can be envious of those who do not put them first. Envy is an emotion that drives a person to want to spoil the good they see because they do not have it. Lastly, they lack empathy for others. They do not see the fact that their child is suffering as a reason to stop their behaviors.

> *Chet was in therapy in his mid-twenties to recover from a childhood of narcissistic abuse by his mother. He recalled his mother criticizing him incessantly for eating too fast, picking his nose, not using correct table manners, leaving his toys out, and so on—anything to keep him off-balance within himself. She bossed him around habitually.*

> *He recalled one episode at age five when he went to McDonald's with his mother and sister. After they finished eating their Happy Meals, his mother curtly told him to "throw this away," referring to the whole table's trash. Chet remembered feeling infuriated at her entitlement to his servitude and knew he had to protest, but in a delicate way. His sharp mind thought he'd fashioned the right response, so when he got back to their table he said, "I cannot wait till I grow up and can boss people around." His mother responded by snarling and squinting, a black look of murderousness in her eyes. In a low, barking tone, she bit off the words, "How dare you say that I boss you around?! After all that I do for you. And this is how you thank me? You are a selfish, mean little brat. I am going to the car. Chet, you sit there and think about that." Chet recalled feeling a searing jolt of shame and wanting to crawl out of his skin. He learned from that moment onward not to speak back to his mother, because her retaliations felt unsurvivable.*

Scapegoating a child (thankfully!) goes against the grain of most of our schemas of parenting, and even humanity. Going out of one's way to blame a child at every turn in order to revel in the sense of (false) superiority one derives from such treatment—and showing no remorse—is antithetical to the meaning of the word "parent."

The Latin root of "parent" is "bringing forth." Parents are responsible for helping their children bring themselves forth into the world, and they can do this in a lot of ways. They may notice and celebrate their child's qualities, take delight in the child's displays of happiness, be available for support as needed, and show interest in what the child thinks, feels, and believes. Those are just a few of the ways in which a child's self can be "parented" into the world.

A child who is scapegoated by a narcissistic parent actually has no parent in the true sense of the word. The child faces an adversary where biology tells them to expect an ally. More insidiously, as a child is prone to believe their parent's cruelty is their fault, the child earmarked for scapegoating faces one of the most unfair of fights. They must both cope with the absence of an adult to help them bring themselves forth and face the searing psychological torment of thinking they're at fault for that absence. Thus, a narcissist gets to land her emotional punches on the child with impunity and great effect.

What Makes a "Good" Scapegoat

In my personal and professional experience, children like Chet who are selected as scapegoats usually stand out. They possess a presence that is palpable to others. They often have a keen sense of fairness and instinctively protest injustice. They are perceptive and can see bad character when it is present. They are usually very empathic and care about others' feelings, and are often protective of people they care about. They can be very intelligent. Most of all, they are tough. When the narcissist chooses a child as a scapegoat, they choose one who can take it. They want to see the child suffer, but not so much that they can't keep hurting them habitually.

> *Chet recalls one noble act that likely sealed his fate as the child to be scapegoated. Despite his younger sister's alliance with his mother, Chet felt protective of her at a young age. On Nancy's birthday, Chet and Nathalie—ages six and three respectively—made Nancy dinner as a present. In the course of making meatballs, they decided to crunch up some graham crackers and put them in the mixture. As they sat down to eat this precociously prepared meal, they giggled with each other. Nathalie asked her mother if she tasted anything different. When Nancy said she did not, Chet and Nathalie laughed harder. Nathalie told her mother, "We put graham cracker crust in them!" Nancy stopped chewing, slammed her fork on the plate, and looked with rage at her daughter. Chet saw this and forcefully exclaimed, "Hey! Stop it! Don't treat her like that. It was just a joke. Why are you so upset?" Nancy looked at Chet and seemed to realize she couldn't continue her planned tirade against Nathalie. Chet felt good that he'd been able to stop her abuse of his sister, even though nobody stood up for him when he was Nancy's target.*

The courage and protectiveness that Chet displayed likely made Nancy aware of how much more he possessed than she did. Her systematic abuse seemed driven by her hatred of him for being a more decent human being than she ever could be. She knew that she was governed by the need to be cruel while he was driven by the need to love and protect.

The Hellish Life of the Scapegoat Child

A scapegoated child knows depths of private suffering that can only be described as hellish. They are born with the biological need for care from people who hate them. It is like being thirsty, and the only person who has water instead gives you sand, then mockingly laughs. The scapegoated child is attacked for trumped-up charges, mercilessly punished, and then denied appeal. They are constantly invalidated in their perspective. The family's goal is to convince the child that they are the sole reason for the family's unhappiness. The child may come to believe that life is only worth living if they can figure out how to not be who they are.

When a child is cast as the enemy in their own family, there is tremendous pressure to turn against themselves. In this case, the scapegoated child has to join in the collective hatred of their existence. At least getting mistreated involves contact.

People who make it through childhood as scapegoats often have to stow away their awareness of their good qualities. The child must hide their own appreciation of who they are, lest they lose whatever connection is available or face even worse abuse. The narcissistic parent wants the scapegoated child to believe they are as horrible as they are being told they are. If the child shows a sense of self-worth or self-possession, the narcissistic parent will take this as an affront to their authority. In essence, the mentality is, *How dare my child think he isn't as bad as I say he is? He must not respect me. I will make him pay.* To avoid this outcome, scapegoated children develop a set of self-devaluing beliefs that keep the narcissistic parent from attacking even harder.

Common Beliefs of Adults Scapegoated as Children

I Am Physically Disgusting

Sometimes scapegoated children are more physically attractive than their narcissistic parent. This simple fact about them can roil the parent. As the child is positively received for his or her looks outside the home, he or she may feel a deep sense of fear and confusion. *Why are people saying I am pretty (or handsome)?* The child may be particularly wary of the narcissist catching wind of this. They likely know that something bad will happen when others tell them they are attractive.

One way for the child to undo the threat posed by his or her good looks is to—unconsciously—distort their perception of the bodily self. An otherwise good-looking kid may decide that he or she is fat, has a big nose, too many pimples, has ugly hair, etc. If the threat of reprisal from the narcissistic parent is great enough, the scapegoated child may simply take such distortions as brute facts. It is not that she *thinks* she's fat, ugly, etc.—she just *is* this way. As uncomfortable as such perceptions are to live with, they are preferable to the cruelty that would ensue if the narcissistic parent felt shown up.

A scapegoat child may go out of their way to appear unattractive. They may wear shabby clothes, decide to bathe less, or stop taking care of their physical fitness. These unconscious strategies comply with the narcissistic parent's insistence that the child think of themselves as worthless. If the child is worthless, then what is the point of caring for their physical appearance?

If I Am Not Being Productive, I Am Worthless

Scapegoated children can find the narcissistic parent's hatred too violent to withstand. One way to cope with the horrific fact that your parent hates you for who you are is to substitute the idea that they hate you for what you do. Making this shift can afford the scapegoated child enough psychological breathing space to go on functioning. This strategy offers hope that the parent might have a change of heart if the child can just "do right." Things do not feel as unfixable.

The drawback is that the scapegoated child is thrust into an endless loop of trying in the face of failure. No matter what the scapegoated child tries—doing his chores perfectly, buying the narcissistic parent a gift, getting good grades, etc.—the parent will ultimately find them to be objectionable. In this system, the child may redouble her efforts to succeed rather than surrender to the horrible reality they face. As adults, they may feel ill at ease when not doing some activity to better themselves in some way or another. Stretches of free time can feel foreboding, as the privilege of enjoying their own company was one their parent actively worked to forbid them.

I Am Always One Mistake Away from Complete Ruin

Scapegoated children often feel like their existence hangs in the balance at each moment. Something final, awful, and dreadful could happen if they make the wrong move. A narcissistic parent who has scapegoated the child is already going to find them to be in the wrong. The ensuing onslaught of yelling, beating, or worse is how they terrorize them. Somewhere inside, the scapegoated child knows that their fate is going to be awful: the narcissistic parent is going to thrash them—it is just a question of when and how. The child must find a way to manage the monumental anxiety they experience in the face of such ongoing threat. One way to do this is to boil down their existence to each moment. No looking forward. No looking backward. Just focusing on what's here right now. The looming dread of what could happen is still there, but it exists more in the shadows. Again, the payoff to this strategy is the ability to go on functioning in the face of the parent's chronic efforts to destroy their quality of life.

It is important to note that boiling everything down to the present moment is different from "being in the now." One can only be mindful when it feels sufficiently safe to do so, and a scapegoated child is not afforded the necessary goodwill and space to be present in that way. Their approach is more like taking a snapshot instead of a video, looking only at this moment rather than how they are being treated over time. To do the latter would bring into awareness how hopelessly mistreated they are and the lack of any viable escape routes.

I Am Defective

A narcissistic parent wants to drill into the scapegoat the notion that he or she is inherently defective. If a child is scapegoated from an early age, he or she may feel a deep sense that there is something wrong with them. Objectively, there is so much right with such children and so much wrong with the narcissistic parent, but that is not what gets internalized for the child. They may have natural social grace or a good sense of humor, but fear social interactions. They may shy away from making friends and later forming romantic relationships out of compliance with what feels like a fundamental truth about themselves. Similarly, they may be athletically gifted but feel overmatched in competitive situations and be unable to utilize their potential.

I Have No Skills or Talents

Scapegoated children are forbidden from knowing what they are good at. To do so would be to defy the narcissist's contention that they are good-for-nothing. Children grow to know that the narcissist will take their possession of skills or talents as an affront to their authority. The belief that they are talentless protects them from the narcissist's envious attacks, and from having something of value—like self-esteem or pride—ripped away by the parent. Managing such losses is a high priority for the scapegoated child, who can only bear so many. A low-level ongoing sense of diminishment is much preferable to the traumatic loss of a cherished sense of self.

If I Disagree, I Will Be Hated and Exiled

This belief is a simple observation for the scapegoated child. The child knows that if he defies the narcissist's claims that he is the source of their unhappiness, he will suffer an even worse fate. Scapegoated children are often threatened with exile from the family, to great unfortunate effect. Despite how torturously the child is treated, the threat of being exiled can feel even worse. Such children learn to present a compliant and agreeable persona to the other family members to avoid their hatred and expulsion. The child must police his impulses, reactions, and perceptions to suppress any expression that could be taken as disagreement.

As adults, scapegoated children may find themselves paralyzed with fear when they consider dissenting in work environments or with their partners. Disagreeing with someone brings them into the forefront. The act delineates the self in stark relief. It is what allows for dialogue in the true sense of the word.

Martin Buber would refer to this as an "I-thou" relationship, where two subjectivities are brought into authentic contact with one another (1970). A person can feel safe to disagree when they can expect to be received with curiosity, non-defensiveness, and responsiveness. Scapegoated children were not afforded such receptions. Instead they had to hide themselves at all times. The bringing forth of themselves that an act of disagreement requires was simply too dangerous.

This coping strategy can lead the scapegoated child to conclude (wrongly) that he or she cares too much about what other people think. In fact, I hear this a lot from adults who were scapegoated as children. Importantly, we all care what others think about us when we disagree.

Some people have had the fortune of believing that others will think good things about them for disagreeing. People who were scapegoated have the misfortune of believing that others will think hateful things about them for disagreeing.

I believe that any human being who expects to be hated and exiled by those they need most would avoid disagreeing with them. In therapy, the task is not to shed the concerns about what others think of them, but rather to consider that people today probably think quite well of them when they disagree. While still caring about what others think, they can find a way to pay attention to the good news that people outside of their family will welcome their perspective, even when it expresses disagreement.

9

How a Narcissistic Family Scapegoats a Child

> *Did you feel like you could do nothing right in your family?*
> *Did you see other kids or siblings get preferential treatment by your parents?*
> *Were you offered affection only when you were sick, disappointed, or depressed?*

This book has addressed the process of narcissistic abuse and how a child is often selected and treated as the scapegoat for the narcissistically abusive parent. The leaves the question of how exactly a narcissistic parent gets the child to identify with the role of scapegoat.

When a child is selected as the source of all the family's problems, it is not enough to blame that child. Effective scapegoating involves influencing the child to believe that they deserve to be blamed because of being so undeserving and/or defective. In this chapter, I explain how inconsistent parenting of the scapegoated child by the narcissistic family is a key element to getting that child to identify as the scapegoat. Such inconsistency can lead the child to conclude that they can do nothing right, do not deserve what other kids deserve, and that they feel closer to Mom or Dad when they act like there is something wrong with them.

Convince the Scapegoat Child That They Can Do Nothing Right

Inconsistent verbal and non-verbal messages are frequently used to undermine the scapegoated child's sense of empowerment and understanding of him- or herself and the world (Vogel & Bell, 1960). Inconsistent messages can take the form of showing indifference toward "negative behavior" at some times, while getting overly punitive for the same behavior at other times. This can lead the child to conclude that no matter what they do, they'll eventually get criticized, so they must deserve it.

> *Jeremy was the scapegoat of his narcissistic family and recalled how family dinners could be torturous for him. By the time he was ten years old, some nights at the dinner table his narcissistic mother would suddenly accuse him of bad table manners, whether it was in the form of supposedly chewing with his mouth open, putting his elbows on the table, or even speaking too loudly. Other nights she paid no attention to his same behavior. As a result, he was always surprised when she attacked him for these acts. It seemed to him like he was being lulled into a false sense of security and then suddenly pounced on.*

Jeremy's experience at the dinner table highlights how inconsistent messaging from his mother about his supposedly problematic behavior prevented him from effectively changing that behavior. If his mother really wanted Jeremy to stop for his own sake, she would have been consistent in her reprimands (of course, they could have been much less harsh) and been pleased when he changed his behavior. Instead, Jeremy had the impression that there was nothing he could have done to stop her from finding fault with his table manners. This contributed to his sense that he could do nothing right.

Convince the Scapegoat Child That They Do Not Deserve What Other Kids Deserve

Here is where double standards come into play. A narcissistic parent may treat the scapegoat child like he or she already gets too much, all while giving that child very little and granting privileges and gifts generously to another child. When this happens, the scapegoat child is led to conclude that they do not deserve what the other child is getting. At first, the scapegoat child will complain and protest at this sort of unfairness. However, such expressions are typically used against the child as evidence that they are selfish and inconsiderate of others' needs, and/or that they take what they do get for granted. Some scapegoated children will stop complaining when met with such humiliating responses and quietly conclude that they do not deserve what the other child—whether sibling, cousin, or someone outside the home—deserves.

> *In therapy, Shayna recalled how her brother had always been treated like a prince in her family, while she always seemed to be a burden and a problem to her parents. She*

started working after school at age fourteen and managed to save up enough money to buy a very cheap and poorly maintained car when she turned sixteen. Meanwhile, her brother, who was three years younger, turned sixteen while she was away at college. One day, she came to home to find that her parents had bought him a late-model sports car despite him never having worked a job or contributed any of his own money. At that point, Shayna was not surprised or ready to protest the unfairness of this galling act of favoritism because she was so conditioned to expect her parents to respond that she was being selfish.

As illustrated by Shayna's story, this tactic involves treating the scapegoated child like they deserve less than other kids and meeting the child's protest with invalidation and attacks on their character. As a result, they learn to tolerate being treated like they are less deserving than the other kids, and eventually they believe it.

Get the Scapegoat Child to Associate Closeness with There Being Something Wrong

When a parent takes special interest in the scapegoat child's emotional or physical ailments, the child can come to associate a sense of closeness with the state of being in disrepair (Pillari, 1991). The narcissistic parent might usually pay very little favorable attention to the scapegoat child, leaving them to suffer a chronic sense of emotional deprivation and loneliness. Those feelings might get relieved temporarily when the narcissistic parent pays special attention to the child's emotional or physical ailments.

Children faced with such emotional deprivation will seek any contact with the parent over no contact. If presenting themselves as sick or unhappy yields the parent's attention then that solves the emptiness they might otherwise experience. The diminishment in self-worth and sacrifice of competence is a sacrifice a child is willing to make for a feeling of connection to the narcissistic parent. This reflects the vulnerability children have as a result of their inborn need to be responded to. That vulnerability is ignored and often exploited by the narcissistic parent.

> *John survived the role of scapegoat in his family. He recalled how his mother would show particular interest in his complexion during his adolescence. She would tell him that she saw pimples on his skin and that he seemed to be developing a bad acne. His doctors would describe his case as mild when he went for treatment, but his mother would insist that it was severe when they got home. Although this led to him feeling self-conscious and embarrassed about his appearance, he nonetheless welcomed the attention she was finally paying him.*

John's case illustrates how a child—even an adolescent—much prefers having a relationship with their parent where they feel bad to no having relationship at all.

How These 3 Tactics Produce the Scapegoat Child

The narcissist often uses a combination of these tactics against the scapegoated child, leaving them feeling like there is no choice but to internalize the idea of who they are that is being imposed upon them by the family. Eventually, the scapegoated child comes to believe that they can do nothing right, that they deserve less than others, and that they only way to get needed responsiveness is show that there is something wrong with them. Once this happens, they may go on to live in a way that complies with the blame and accusations thrust upon them by the narcissistic family.

Of course, those of you reading this have been able to preserve a part of yourselves that knew—or wanted to know—otherwise. Somehow or another, you held out hope that you could live as you actually are rather than having to comply with these artificial messages about who you are.

10

The Scapegoat's Confusion

> *Do you wonder whether your parent actually good to you, but you have somehow failed to see it?*
> *Do you question whether you are being cruel and wrong by thinking of this parent as someone who has hurt you?*
> *Do you doubt whether you can trust your own perceptions and judgments?*

In this chapter, I explain why a narcissistic parent's attempts to invalidate your reality can feel so undermining. There are good reasons for this, and understanding them can empower you.

Why It Can Be Hard to Believe Yourself over the Narcissistic Abuser

If you have survived narcissistic abuse—particularly in the role of scapegoat—you may have had to believe you were defective in order to share a reality with your narcissistic parent. This may have taken the form of the narcissistic abuser expressing bewilderment at your opinions or ideas in order to convey the message that your judgment was poor.

Later, when you expressed a feeling, you may have been met with recoil or the accusation that you couldn't control your emotions. The narcissistic abuser may have worked to influence other family members and friends to react to and think of you similarly—or worse. In the end, a scapegoat survivor who is treated this way often has to assume a pseudo-identity of being "pathological" or "crazy."

When such a systematic effort to invalidate, devalue, and undermine your standing is in place, protest will only result in exasperation and despair. Many survivors have come to the harrowing conclusion that there is nothing they can say or do or "clear up" to convince the narcissistic abuser of their good intentions. There is a different kind of calculus being used, one where the survivor has to be found as defective—nothing else can or will be considered.

As you have learned in previous chapters, the narcissistic abuser's way of coping with their own (usually unconscious) sense of worthlessness is to deny it and relocate those feelings into someone else—often the scapegoat child. Next, that narcissist acts in ways that influence the scapegoat target to adopt these feelings of worthlessness as his or her own. The narcissistic parent's efforts to undermine your judgment and perceptions serves the psychological function of relocating their own worthlessness into you. That may be one reason why it can feel impossible to "clear up" their distorted view of you. There is just too much at stake for them.

So, if you're in a position where the first priority is for someone else to be there, and the hope that that person treats you well comes second, then there is no other choice but to comply with the narcissistic abuser's claims that you are defective. This position literally applies to children of a narcissistic parent. As it is often said, our order of preference is a good relationship, bad relationship, then no relationship. We have to avoid the third alternative at all costs.

The rub in having to comply with the narcissistic abuser's claims of your defectiveness is that these claims are not true. So, in order to maintain an attachment by sharing a reality with this person, you must create a false reality within that goes along with the narcissistic abuser's narrative of who you are and who they are.

George Orwell's *1984* is a great book about the experience of living in a totalitarian state. When I read it in high school, I was blown away by how plainly Orwell described the mind-tricks played on the followers of the dictator in this state (which for our purposes we might easily swap out for the term narcissistic abuser). The main character, Winston Smith, begins questioning all the loyalty practices he is being forced to participate in, one of which is what the dictatorship calls doublethink:

> *To forget whatever it was necessary to forget, then to draw it back into memory again at the moment when it was needed, and then promptly to forget it again, and above all, to apply the same process to the process itself—that was the ultimate subtlety: consciously to induce unconsciousness, and then, once again, to become unconscious of the act of hypnosis you had just performed. Even to understand the word—doublethink—involved the use of doublethink. (Orwell, 1949)*

I think this perfectly describes the process of what the scapegoat has to do to go along with the narcissistic abuser's claims that his or her judgment is defective.

> *Shannon came to treatment to overcome the effects of her narcissistic mother's abuse. Her natural reactions had always been to care about the feelings of others and seek to connect with them. In high school, she heard about an organization called Habitat for Humanity where volunteers went to construction sites to help build houses for families in need. She started attending and made friends with some of the other volunteers. Unfortunately, Shannon's narcissistic mother experienced Shannon's genuine enjoyment of connecting with others as a threat to her own artificially inflated sense of self-worth.*
>
> *One Saturday when Shannon returned from the construction site, tired but satisfied with her day's efforts and camaraderie she got to enjoy with the crew, her mother came storming into the living room where she was sitting. She furiously accused Shannon of shirking her household duties so she could go off and play "do-gooder" to others. Next, she told Shannon that she knew the real her and wasn't fooled by what she was trying play off to others.*

Shannon had to find a way to believe what her mother was telling her, and I think that process of doublethink is exactly what often happens in these situations. She knew on some level that her inclination to help others was genuine, yet she had to believe the opposite message she received from her mother—that her desire to help others was insincere and manipulative. So, she had to be aware of her impulses to help others, then quickly change her opinion on what those impulses meant, reinterpreting them in line with her mother's claims. She might say something to herself like, "There I go again, trying to look good to others by helping them."

In order to stay in some kind of relationship with her narcissistically abusive mother, Shannon had to forget that the perception of herself as manipulative had started with her mother's tirade. That's what Winston Smith means when he says doublethink involves "consciously to induce unconsciousness, and then, once again, to become unconscious of the act of hypnosis you had just performed." In essence, someone like Shannon has to forget her mother's claims and see them as her own opinion.

Shannon and people in her position have to deliberately stop believing themselves in order to believe what's necessary to survive. In recovery, this is why it can make you as a survivor wonder, *Am I making all this up?* when your efforts to set boundaries and create needed distance from a narcissistic abuser are met with incredulousness and attacks.

11

The Scapegoat's Mental Frame

> *Do you find it difficult to enjoy doing what you are good at?*
>
> *Is it impossible not to be self-conscious when doing something you know you like to do?*
>
> *Are you unaware of what you are good at (even if you are successful)?*

Someone who had survived narcissistic abuse as the scapegoat in his family of origin recently described what it was like for him to play his favorite sport—basketball. We'll call this person Steph (no relation to Curry). Steph had loved shooting baskets and playing pickup games with his friends since he was five years old. Something just felt good and right to him and in his body when he was on the basketball court.

However, Steph's experience at home was completely the opposite: he felt like an unwelcome alien among his parents and siblings, and he always had to watch his back to see what he would be accused of that might get him into trouble. As such, he lived in two wildly divergent realities: being dehumanized and blamed for any and everything in his family versus being appreciated by his teammates for being able to pass and score so well on the court. The inner experience Steph described himself as feeling when he played basketball shows how he dealt with this predicament:

> I always think I am going to make a mistake on the court. It is a surprise to me every time I do something well. Sometimes, I am amazed at how different the track in my head is compared to what I am actually doing on the court. It is really hard to reflect on my skills as a basketball player and my accomplishments. I fear that if I think too much about what I can do, then I won't be able to do it anymore. I'll think of some problem in my shooting or passing and obsess over it, and it'll ruin my game.

Steph has a mental frame about who he is that opposes how he is actually living his life. The American Psychological Association defines a mental frame as "a set of rules . . . by which an individual perceives and evaluates the world." In this chapter, I describe what it is like to have to live with a mental frame that is incongruent with how you actually live in the world. Next, I'll explain how surviving narcissistic abuse as the scapegoat can bring this about.

Why It Can Feel So Bad to Do What You're Good At

An experience like Steph's, where what was happening on the basketball court diverged greatly from the narrative of what was happening in his mind, can be common after surviving narcissistic abuse as the scapegoat. You may find yourself to be very competent at work or school yet constantly tell yourself that you're one mistake away from ruining it all.

Or maybe you are told that you are a very good friend, parent, and/or partner, yet you always feel like you're one step away from betraying, disappointing, or failing the people you love.

The conviction that one is not as good as one seems to be is not easy to give up. This experience can understandably frustrate scapegoat survivors. It also makes fraught the experience of doing what you are good at. Although Steph loved basketball, the experience of playing always carried with it a state of anxiety, unease, and even mild depression that he had to tolerate in order to play. In order to survive narcissistic abuse as the scapegoat, it is typically necessary to adopt a mental frame about who you are in the world that corresponds to the distorted and devaluing messages you receive from your family. There is pressure from within and without to do this.

At the same time, the scapegoat child has to go on living—and does. In the process, they will show who they actually are in the world, and at times encounter accurate feedback about themselves. These moments are where the mental frame needed to survive at home often becomes most conspicuous. One client remembered winning spelling bees in his second-grade class week after week, then telling his friends at lunch that he was "stupid." His friends were upset to hear him say this, but he was being treated as though he was unimportant and a problem by his narcissistic mother at home, and the feelings of esteem and pride brought on by his talent in spelling made him confused. As this client went on to succeed in school, he described it as a very tension-filled experience, because he'd be studying on top of this mental frame about himself that said he was stupid.

12

The Worst Parts About Being the Scapegoat

> *Do you feel a gnawing emptiness and/or sadness that seems to have always been there?*
> *Do you feel apart from others and confused about how to belong?*
> *Do you have to fight a feeling of hopelessness that casts a shadow over your life?*

I once saw the comic Bill Burr perform, and he talked about being on psychedelic mushrooms with his friends. Now if you know much about him, he alludes being from a family where yelling and unpredictable outbursts of rage from his father were just a part of growing up. I don't know if either of his parents were narcissistic or not, but for me, the experience he described having while on mushrooms highlights the worst part about being the scapegoat child to a narcissistically abusive parent.

Burr said that, when the shrooms hit him, he went to a place that felt very dark and that nothing he thought or said to himself would change that feeling . . . it just was. He went to his room in order not to rain on his friends' parade, and the feeling did not change. He was struggling against it, but nothing worked. He went to hold his wife's hand, and it did not comfort him. He said that he felt lonely and unloved and finally stopped trying to fight it. Then he realized that this was exactly how he'd felt throughout his whole childhood.

What stood out to me about this part of his act—it was a great show, and it is a testament to his genius that he could weave such a harrowing vignette into an hour of comedy—was how he described the experience of there being someone there, but connecting to them provided him with no comfort. He had gone to hold his wife's hand and felt nothing in doing so. That experience gets at the heart of the trauma faced by the scapegoat child to a narcissistic parent.

The child learns deep down that they have a parent there, but that going to that parent offers no felt comfort, protection, or sense of safety. Thus, in that they are around people in a physical sense but cannot feel an inner connection to them, the child is catastrophically alone. And they have to suffer their aloneness privately—just as Bill Burr did on his mushroom trip.

In this chapter, I explain why the scapegoated child of the narcissistic parent often endures this trauma of having nobody who can help him feel better inside. Next, I want to offer some thoughts about what to do when or if this state arises in the process of recovering from narcissistic abuse.

Loneliness and Unloveability

Let's quickly review the psychological dynamics in play when a narcissistic parent identifies a child to play the role of scapegoat. The narcissist starts with a core sense of worthlessness that they cannot bear to acknowledge, and so has to relegate it to their unconscious. Next, the narcissist works—again unconsciously—to discover this worthlessness in someone else, usually someone whom they have authority over, or where there is a power imbalance in the relationship favoring the narcissist. Third, the narcissist acts in ways to coercively influence the other person to identify with their cast-off feelings of worthlessness. So, the narcissist may overtly or covertly undermine, criticize, invalidate, deride, or otherwise hurt the other person, but in a way designed to get them to believe they deserve to be treated this way—that is, to become the scapegoat. That it is the other person's flawed-ness that makes it necessary for the narcissist to treat them this way.

The child is likely going to learn that getting closer to the narcissistic parent brings them no comfort or reassurance. No, the scapegoat child is very much on their own in life, and must find a way to manage the panic, terror, anger, and despair that this cruel fact can evoke in them.

It can feel like an endless permanent state of being lonely and unloved from which there is no rescue. The child is biologically programmed to see the narcissistic parent as the only person who can rescue them from this state of utter aloneness, yet feels the utter absence of love, kindness, and care from them. It goes without saying that the narcissistic parent cannot also offer kindness, respect, care and curiosity while they're using the child to rid themselves of a feeling they cannot tolerate. Unfortunately, the child has to bear the cost of parent putting his or her psychological pathology first.

The narcissistic parent's structural lack of empathy for others helps them do this without concern for the consequences to the child. I believe that this is sensed by the child, and part of what seals their fate—that appealing to the narcissistic parent's concern for their well-being will do no good. The child has a parent standing there, but no connection is coming from them—a horrifying reality to cope with at a time in life when they do not yet have the inner resources to cope. The child cannot say, "Whoa, what's that parent's problem? I'm outta here—I'm gonna go where I am wanted." Instead, they must stay, trying to eke out some connection in spite of the hopelessness they feel about ever getting it.

Hopelessness

There is a profound dashing of hopes for the child who suffers narcissistic abuse from a parent. As I mentioned, a child is biologically programmed to be hopeful that his parent will provide him with what he needs to feel securely attached, love him for the separate person he is, and that the love he has to offer is valuable to that parent. None of these hopes are realized by the scapegoat child to a narcissistic parent. As a result, he faces a hopeless situation, and the feeling that often accompanies hopelessness is despair. So, the scapegoat child may be very accustomed to an inner—often very private—sense of despair at the felt hopelessness of there being no one out there who can offer them the sense of connection they are seeking.

This post-traumatic sense of hopelessness can also make it feel dangerous to entertain hope. For the scapegoat survivor, it can feel threatening to consider that new people might be able to offer a connection that can be felt. The task in recovery from such trauma involves integrating what you have been through with what might now be possible. There is no denying—only accepting—what you have faced at the hands of your narcissistic parent. And it can be in the case of accepting this that the notion of hope can re-emerge and be tolerated.

It can be very important to do this work while in therapy, because it offers a specific kind of relationship that allows you to describe what you have been through and what you've suffered while being compassionately understood and validated. You and your therapist get to work together on how your past hopelessness might be getting in the way of finding connections that feel good in your current relationships. The initial problem was the lack of connection offered by your narcissistic parent, so it can be very important to successfully come to terms with that experience while experiencing a connection with someone. That can be very healing to the initial trauma of being and feeling alone and unloved.

Another resource to help with accepting what the scapegoat survivor has lived through is my online course on recovery from narcissistic abuse[3]. This course offers seven video modules that cover in more depth the three pillars of recovery. I identify challenges faced in each of the pillars and offer actionable strategies for overcoming these challenges. Lastly, there is an accompanying private Facebook group where you can connect with other survivors and know you are not alone.

---

[3] The course can be found here: https://lp.jreidtherapy.com/narcissistic-abuse-course

It is like the scapegoated child who is suffering this experience is in a maze with no way out. You can think of recovery as seeing the dead end of the maze you were in—this time from outside the maze and while in connection to someone new. That way, you know you're not still in the maze and it is safe to entertain hope that you can find your way out and that you are no longer alone.

I hope this chapter has shed some light on an the wordless but extremely painful aspect of having to endure the role of the scapegoat child. As with all traumas, finding language for what was once wordless pain and communicating that pain to safe other people is an essential step to healing from it.

13

Narcissistic Abuse Means Always Having to Say You're Sorry

> *Did your safety depend on getting your narcissistic parent to accept your apologies?*
> *Do you often worry about having offended people?*
> *If a conflict happens in your relationship, do you expect to be the one at fault?*

Many scapegoat survivors are familiar with having to frequently offer apologies while rarely receiving them in return. There may be a good reason for this. A big part of narcissistic abuse can be the absence of protection from it by anyone else. When you are selected as the scapegoat to a narcissistic abuser and there is nobody around who intervenes on your behalf, you must find a way to protect yourself. Trying to fight the narcissistic abuser will not work, since the scapegoat, being a child, is in a less powerful position.

Fleeing the narcissist doesn't work, either. The scapegoat can feel like the narcissist has what they desperately need to exist happily, convinced that they have to win their narcissistic parent's approval before they can value their own self. If the child flees, they are giving up trying to get what they so desperately need from the parent.

So what's left?

Figuring out a way to get the narcissistic abuser to relent on their attacks on you, the scapegoat. And what's a very good way to do this? Developing the reflex to apologize for any and everything that leads to the narcissistic parent's unhappiness.

In this chapter, I want to explain how and why narcissistic abuse can mean always having to say you're sorry. I hope that this explanation can yield a compassionate—and accurate—narrative of how this coping strategy developed out of an utter lack of protection from abuse that you did not deserve. The reflex to over-apologize was a means to the end of finding protection where no other kind existed. Over time, alternate forms of protection can be established so that you can feel safe enough to experiment with not apologizing—or being ready to apologize—as much. If you read until the end, I'll offer a concrete way of doing just this: taking a specific action to offer yourself a greater sense of protection so that you get to apologize to people of your choosing *only* when you mean it.

The Fallacy That It Is Always the Scapegoat Child's Fault

Recently, I was talking to a friend who was also a scapegoat in his family. I asked where he stood with a sibling who always seemed to find fault with him. He said something to the effect of, "Sometimes you just have to question how it can be possible that I am *always* in the wrong? Like, statistically speaking."

This exchange really got me thinking about the falseness of the scapegoat always having to be the one to apologize for a supposed fault. Finding flaws to always exist in the scapegoat is necessary for the narcissist to feel safe from their awareness of their own perceived flaws. If the scapegoat is not always wrong, then maybe they are not suitable for offloading the narcissist's own worthlessness. That could make it boomerang back on the narcissist, which would feel intolerable to them. As such, the scapegoat may feel pressure to be and stay wrong so that the narcissist does not have to experience what—for them—would be the catastrophe of being in the wrong.

Importantly, through all of this, no one else is protesting how the narcissistic abuser is treating the scapegoat survivor and intervening to protect the scapegoat. The scapegoat child is being treated this way against the backdrop of being completely alone in this mess.

How Apologizing Protects the Scapegoat

Once the narcissistic parent has cast the child as the receptacle for their own worthlessness, and no one else offers that child protection, the child learns that being wrong is a condition for feeling connected. Being wrong is what happens when they try to engage with others and/or the world. It is a matter of when, not if, they anger or disappoint someone else—feel deserving of that reaction—and must offer an apology. The apology often results in a diminishment in the intensity of the attack and felt shame, guilt, and self-loathing that the scapegoat is often left with.

First and foremost, the narcissistic parent needs to feel right. Being right for the narcissist gives their very fragile sense of self-worth a boost—albeit temporarily. When there is not another parent willing to stand up for the scapegoat child, it is in that child's best interest to keep the narcissistic parent feeling right. What better way to do this than to offer an apology for whatever complaint the parent has?

One of the most dangerous scenarios for the scapegoat is when they take some type of action, and the narcissistic abuser characterizes that action as having rightfully caused their anger and contempt. They argue that the scapegoat's behavior was disrespectful, hurtful, or deceptive. For the scapegoat, this means that something that emanated from their Self is being held up as the reason for the narcissistic abuser's vicious attack. This can feel very threatening to the child's core self. It can even feel like the core self may not survive. Having an apology at the ready can feel like a much needed "take-back," where the scapegoat can rebuke themselves doing what they did and often reduce the intensity of the narcissist's attack.

When the Narcissistic Abuser Tells You That You Don't Really Mean It

When they apologize to their narcissistic abuser, scapegoat survivors are often very familiar with being told that they don't really mean it. When this happens, the narcissist may go on to further denigrate the scapegoat for being deceptive along with whatever the initial "offense" was. This is a terrible position to be in for the scapegoat, because now the apology is no longer working—it has somehow made the narcissist more angry, and therefore dangerous. When this happens, all that is left is for the scapegoat to just get to the other side of the attack, endure all the venom, and hope that they are not psychologically destroyed by it.

I'd like to offer some explanation as to why you may have felt guilty of accusations that you did not really mean your apologies. All of this is a ruse—the narcissist's fictional attempt to deny their own feelings of worthlessness—so whatever comes from it will reek of inauthenticity in one way or another.

Thus, there is truth in the claim that you didn't really mean your apology. It's not that the scapegoat is trying to be deceptive, but rather that the narcissist's entire blaming of the scapegoat is the primary act of deceit. It is a deceit of reality and a deceit of the narcissist's own self-experience. They are telling themselves a lie and forcing others to go along with it—via the narcissist's privileged position in the relationship—so that they can believe the lie a bit more.

When you feel bad or guilty for not feeling more remorseful for supposedly hurting or disrespecting your narcissistic parent, take comfort in knowing that you don't really feel sorry because there was nothing to really be sorry for.

14

Feeling Unreal After Narcissistic Abuse

> *Do you sometimes feel like you are watching your life from outside yourself?*
> *When you think about your past, does it seem like you weren't really there?*
> *Do you find it impossible to pay attention to your own experience when interacting with others?*

One of the grave impacts of being scapegoated by a narcissistic parent is the sense that, at your core, you are not real. Survivors often feel this way from early in life and have found a way to live with it. This can be a terrifying feeling that is often not discussed with friends, partners, therapists, or even yourself.

In this chapter, I will explain how kids typically develop a sense of being uniquely real in the world. Accurate recognition from and idealization of good-enough parents is necessary in order to feel real. These ingredients are not available for the scapegoat child of a narcissistic parent. Last, I will cover how therapy can help the survivor recover a sense of being real.

Recognition Helps Us Feel Real

In my opinion, the problem of feeling real traces back to how accurately recognized we felt—or didn't feel—during our upbringing. Each of us has a unique set of attributes or ways of being that correspond to who we are in the world. When one of those aspects of who were are gets noticed by someone else, we feel more real in the world, particularly if that someone else matters to us.

How It Is Supposed to Work

Think about why it feels good to hear someone tell you, "OK, I see you!" Let's say Sharone is an eighth grader in her social studies class. Her favorite teacher, Mr. Turner, is having a discussion on the American Civil Rights Movements during the 1950s and '60s. Sharone raises her hand and says, "It seems like today's BLM protests are using similar tactics as Gandhi's and MLK's nonviolent protests. Both are and were trying to turn the hearts of the onlookers to see the injustice."

Mr. Turner pauses and says, "OK, Sharone, I see you. That is a great point. Class, what are some of the overlapping features of today's protests and the philosophy of nonviolent protest developed by Gandhi, then MLK?" Sharone feels very *real* in this moment. She's made a contribution to the class that was all her own. Someone she admires recognized and valued that contribution. Sharone has the sense that she is more at home in her own skin, proud to be who she is, and like her voice matters.

When we are recognized for who we uniquely are, we transition seamlessly from being passive to being active in the world. Sharone took a risk by actively sharing something of herself. She could not have predicted with 100 percent certainty that Mr. Turner would respond the way he did. She knew him well enough to expect him to do so, and that predictability made it feel way less risky to raise her hand. This predictability of how she will be responded to affords her a sense of continuity of herself and others. Sharone walks around with the general belief that others appreciate and respect her opinion. She has grown to expect to feel pride when she speaks up in the world.

How It Is Not Supposed to Work

Luis was born to a narcissistic mother. She was a social worker and had curated an image of being a selfless caregiver to their community. With Luis, however, she incessantly criticized him for almost everything he did or said.

One typical episode occurred when he was five years old. He was on the playground, and his mother saw another mother who she was friends with. She started talking to this woman, and Luis remembers feeling like they were talking about him. His mother then called him over and asked him to say hello. Luis remembers feeling nervous because he did not understand what his mother was up to. After greeting his mother's friend, he quickly picked his nose—as he usually did when he was nervous—and ran back to the swing set.

On the car ride home, Luis was in the backseat, the black eyes of his mother peering at him in the rearview mirror. She was staring at him intermittently and finally said, "Luis, you really embarrassed me by picking your nose like that in front of that woman. I didn't know what to say to her. After you left, I could tell she was completely disgusted by you. You better stop doing that!" Luis recalled feeling a hot flush of shame and wanting to fall through the car seat, through the paved road to somewhere he could never be found.

Luis's template for what to expect when he was met in the world was very different from Sharone's. He learned to expect derision, humiliation, and rebuke. He was a smart, dignified, and kindhearted person, so the reception he got from his mother was not only cruel, but also inaccurate. Thus, when she responded in such critical ways toward him, he would feel profoundly unreal. She was blaming him for being someone he simply was not. At such a young age, he could not discern this fact. He trusted his mother's authority and assumed that she saw something in him that he didn't. The truth was that his mother was engaged in a gross act of projecting her own sense of worthlessness onto him. It was not until he sought therapy in adulthood that he grew wise to this.

Mirroring and Idealization in the Healthy Family

A sense of realness in the world really speaks to the question of how intact your Self feels. Children require certain patterns of responses from certain figures to consolidate their sense of Self. In fact, eventual narcissists are thought to experience deficits in this kind of needed responsiveness.

Psychoanalytic theorist Heinz Kohut posits that children have two critical ongoing needs for being recognized by their parents. First, the child's original expressions of himself must be acknowledged and credited to who that child uniquely is. Kohut referred to this as "empathic mirroring." Imagine a three-year-old named Zion who tests very high in the sensorimotor and muscle coordination tests for his age. While he is in the living room on a lazy Saturday afternoon, he crawls across the carpet to get a ball he wants to play with. As he's crawling, his dad bellows, "Fast, Zion!" and Zion feels the charge of getting noticed for who he really is. He may not have language yet, but he knows deeply that when he acts from the center of himself, he usually is recognized and affirmed.

The second critical need is for a child to have someone to look up to and admire who also sees them as special. Kohut referred to this as "idealization." In short, the child needs someone for whom he genuinely wants to be a "chip off of the old block." The adult has to be able to offer qualities that are important to the child, so that the child takes delight in being associated with that adult. It is particularly important that the adult genuinely possess these qualities. Otherwise, the child may have to lie to himself to find someone to fit this critical role. When a good-enough parent can offer enough mirroring and warrants the child's idealization, over time the child internalizes these experiences and forms as sense of unique realness within.

What Happens in a Narcissistic Family

Now let's look at what can happen when a child is born into a narcissistic family. In such cases, the child's need for mirroring and idealization get subverted in ways that leave the child in a chronic state of dishonesty and feeling unrecognized to himself.

The "Black Mirror" for the Scapegoat Child of the Narcissist

The scapegoat child becomes the receptacle into which the narcissistic parent relocates their own selfishness, unreliability, and lack of integrity. In contrast, the child is looking for a parent to accurately recognize them and affirm their unique ways of being. The narcissistic parent and child are at complete odds with one another.

When the narcissistic parent's need to relocate competes with the child's need to be mirrored, power will always break the tie—and the narcissistic parent ultimately holds all the power and authority. The child is forced to sacrifice their need.

> *Many survivors of narcissistic parents recall being told they did not care about their own family when they wanted to spend time with their friends in adolescence. Gus grew up with an altruistic narcissistic father who curated an image of himself as a self-sacrificing patriarch. Gus was naturally funny, affable, and drew people to him. His father would relentlessly scapegoat Gus at home for being lazy, selfish, and more interested in being popular than helping out around the house. Gus had a strong sense of integrity and felt*

humiliated when his father accused him of being a social climber without regard for his family.

At age fourteen, Gus was invited to play street hockey with some older friends from high school. He was excited, but tried not to show this to his father, because that might make his father say no all the more. As usual, Gus was given a long list of cleaning chores to do, and he did them. When he was about to go to the game, his father said, "Wait! I have to inspect how well you cleaned." Gus clenched up inside. This was not good. His father lifted the toilet seat and claimed to see an area that Gus had missed. He slammed the seat down and began screaming at his son for "being more interested in going out to have fun than doing what his family needed him to do." Needless to say, Gus was forbidden from going to the game.

Gus's actual qualities of being sociable, athletic, and charismatic were absolutely not mirrored by his father. Instead, his father fed Gus a completely distorted view of himself as selfish and inconsiderate. The implication was that his father "really knew" what Gus was like, and if his friends had known, they would have reacted in the same way. This confused Gus—he could not figure out what was real about him. Was he the likable guy his friends treated him as? Or was he the self-absorbed jerk his father insisted he was?

A scapegoated child who possesses actual good qualities must bear the burden of being received in a way that is not aligned with how he actually is inside. In the example above, Luis's instincts skewed toward kindness, protection, and care, and yet he lived in a world where his narcissistic mother claimed to experience him as self-absorbed, disgusting, and ill-mannered. It is not difficult to see how he might have a hard time experiencing himself as real. He had to act like he was who he was being told he was, yet he knew that at his core, it didn't fit him. It is a remarkable feat that children like Luis find a way to endure such a private, ongoing hell.

These kinds of stories can and do have good endings. Once these children are out of the narcissist's environment, they can find people who accurately see them for who they are, and therapy can help untangle the false mirroring messages they received. A sense of realness can be achieved—even if it's a bit delayed.

Having to Falsely Idealize a Narcissistic Parent

Now let's look at the predicament for the child who has to idealize a narcissistic parent. It is easy to see how gratifying it could be for such a parent to have a child who looks admiringly up at him and is willing to do whatever he tells her. The parent's grandiosity and entitlement are well met when the child is idealizing him. The problem can occur when the child moves away from her idealizing stance toward the parent, expressing a will of her own or paying attention to herself more than the parent. In these cases, the parent's sense of entitlement feels grossly violated, and severe punishment can ensue.

> *Mario survived a sadistic and narcissistic father. In the first five years of his life, he remembers being treated like his father's special little friend. He looked up to him, and his father seemed to look fondly upon and after Mario. In*

therapy, we determined that something changed profoundly when Mario started to develop into his own person.

His father would seek out opportunities to put him in scary situations. Mario disturbingly recalled being told—at age six—that they were locked out of the house. His father told him to squeeze into a crawl space in order to unlock the cellar door from the inside. That crawl space was thought to contain rats and bats, and Mario was naturally terrified. As he later reflected on that incident, he realized that his father could have just opened the cellar doors through another entrance. Mario realized that his father had been seeking to put him in a terrifying situation out of sheer cruelty.

The child of a narcissistic parent who breaks the idealizing stance can encounter the terror of the parent's resulting rage. The parent will often feel entitled to the child's idealization, and a child who moves his attention from the parent to himself is failing to meet this expectation. When the narcissist's entitlement is not complied with, they may experience their core sense of worthlessness. As with Mario's father, the narcissist will take swift and cruel action to punish the "offender" and restore their compliance. The narcissist must do this to keep avoiding how worthless they feel.

It is important to appreciate the danger the child is put in when they stop authentically idealizing the narcissistic parent. Rage—or worse—is likely to ensue. In order to survive such an upbringing, a kid may wisely conclude that it is best to keep idealizing the narcissistic parent. They may learn to avoid feelings, perceptions, or ways of being that encourage them to see the parent plainly. That is, the child may structure their lives so that they feel convinced of the correctness in continuing to idealize the dangerous parent. The result can be a core feeling that they are being dishonest with themselves. It is indeed dishonest, but this is not the result of a weak character. Rather, being dishonest about the falsely idealized narcissistic parent is the *only* way the kid can survive their parenting.

In essence, the child's natural need to idealize a strong caregiver gets hijacked to minimize the damage done by the narcissistic parent. The child of the narcissistic parent is forced to use his inner and outer real estate to feed the parent's grandiosity and entitlement—or else. His own need to idealize can make this process feel less enslaving. He may feel as though he is getting something in return by continuing to see the parent as worthy of idealization. The hope this offers the child can be integral to having the will to keep on going. Once the danger of childhood has passed, the opportunity presents itself to undo the lies fueled by the forced idealization of the narcissistic parent.

Falsely idealizing the narcissistic parent contributes to the difficulty the child has in feeling real. Their need to idealize a parent who is deserving, and non-possessive about this need, goes unmet. Instead, the child creates an artificial drama in their mind that imbues someone woefully short of idealizable qualities with a surplus of them. The child can end up feeling like there is nothing solid within or without to look up to. They may lose hope that good qualities *actually* exist in themselves and others. All of these experiences contribute to the feeling of being unreal.

15

Surviving Narcissistic Abuse in Childhood

> *Is it profoundly uncomfortable when someone else notices you or something positive about you?*
> *Is it nearly impossible to ignore the needs of others in favor of your own?*
> *Do you feel purposeless when you are not doing something for someone else?*

A very wise client of mine—Mario—identified his goal in therapy in our first session as being to "not care so much what other people think." He'd survived a childhood with a narcissistic father who sadistically enjoyed making him suffer. Mario lamented how he found himself feeling preoccupied with what other people *might* think negatively about him. He would find himself racked with anxiety to the point of paralysis when trying to write an email to a colleague. Mario's heightened anxiety initially felt like a character flaw to him. "Why am I so dependent on others' approval?" he would exclaim.

In this chapter, I describe how scapegoat child victims of narcissistic abuse have to shift all of their attention outside of themselves to survive. In their childhood homes, these children face a danger that never goes away. Mom or Dad is abusive while neglecting the child's needs, while the enabler parent makes themselves unavailable to the child via withdrawal or participating in the abuse.

The Scapegoat Child Is All Alone

Scapegoat children often go unprotected by bystanders to the narcissistic parent's abuse, which may lead to them feeling disconnected. They understandably conclude that they are all alone in the world and singularly deserving of their family's abuse. They have been forced to seek protection and felt security from people inclined to make them suffer. In order to remain willing to seek out such scary parents, they must sequester the parts of themselves that want to run away and hide or fight back. As part of this Faustian bargain, these children lose a sense of kindredness to the human condition. They often feel like they are unique and "just different" from everyone else. That is certainly how their families treat them, and this gets transferred to how they assume the rest of the world understands them.

The child is in a heightened state of fear at the inevitability of the narcissistic parent's abuse. They feel helpless to protect themselves because the enabler parent does not have their back. When overwhelming stress is guaranteed but surviving it is not, all organisms face an existential crisis. Is it worth it to continue living when life feels so torturous? Yet some children have the inner resiliency to fight on in spite of such no-immediate-win circumstances.

Leaving Oneself

For the scapegoat child, fighting on means shifting all of his attention to the people and things around him, and directing attention away from himself. Such children are often attacked based on who they are to the narcissistic parent, not what they did or did not do. It is often the children who have innate good qualities that draw the envy-based hatred of narcissistic parents. The child can then conclude that being connected to who he is only puts him closer to the annihilating agony of being hated by the person who's supposed to love and protect him the most. Words cannot convey how toxic and—for a child—unsurvivable such parental hatred can feel. The child must go on without feeling it, or perish.

> Kevin was a client who came to therapy because he wanted to develop more of a personal life. The only time he wasn't anxious was when he was at work, and the rest of his life felt empty. We grew to understand that his mother was narcissistic, with a bent toward sadism, and his father lacked empathy for his children while seeking only to please his wife. Kevin's younger sister was indoctrinated into the system of targeting him as the problem child. In his family, being awake meant being in danger.
>
> In Kevin's case, there was a moralistic quality to the incessant criticism and abuse. He would be screamed at to get his elbows off the table when eating, to stop picking his nose as a four-year-old, to not eat so fast, to pick up his toys, etc. All of these excuses for his mother's scorn and contempt toward him seemed justified, as if all the yelling and derision would stop if he simply did all the things he was being told to

do. This led him to conclude that he made his family unhappy and that he deserved their hostility.

Early in Kevin's life, this experience brought panic and a fear of not being able to go on psychologically and emotionally. At the same time, he had to continue to live with the people who were hurting him and behave as if things were normal. When he was in first grade, he would brace himself when his mother came to tuck him into bed. He had to act like she was a good mother and that he appreciated her. Once she left his room, Kevin lay there with the terrifying knowledge of how alone and trapped he felt. To escape these feelings and be able to keep going, he would stare intently at a stack of board games in his open closet. There was a way that one of the rectangular boxes seemed to magically turn into the adjacent game. It was a kind of optical illusion that allowed him to wonder about it instead of himself. He would focus entirely on these board games and feel a numbness come over him. That numbness was so welcome because it gave him his first taste of relief from the constant state of feeling threatened and trapped.

From that moment on, Kevin would focus on others and his environment as much as possible. This tactic served two purposes: 1) it afforded him relief from knowing how much danger he was in, and 2) it kept him focused on the fluctuations in his mother's mood so that he might anticipate and reduce the damage of her eventual rage when she released it at him. There is a tragedy in this kind of solution for a child, because he loses the one person who could offer him a real escape—himself. By focusing solely on the danger of his mother and other family members, he lost the *knowledge of who he actually was, how undeserving he was of their contempt, and what he could do to defend himself. Instead, when her rage kicked his goal in was to return her to a state of neutrality toward him.*

This is why parental narcissistic abuse can be so damaging to a child. When getting mistreated, Kevin's goal was to get his mother to like him again, rather than to fight or flee her abuse. When that feels like the only tactic available, it is like the child is trapped with a tiger. The notion of a future becomes impossible, because it just means more misery. Clear-eyed assessments of his past are also too horrifying to make. All that's left is now—this moment—and getting through it. It is essential for the child in this predicament to narrow his attention to the present. Otherwise, he risks collapsing from the despair of knowing what has been done to him by his abusive family and what they likely have in store for him.

The Narcissistic Parent Seeks to Poison the Child's Self-Regard

When a child is thrust into the companionless world of being the family's scapegoat and learns to leave himself, he may work to deny his own existence to himself. Such children, and later adults, are often intensely attuned to the thoughts and feelings of others.

As described earlier in this chapter, the advantage of leaving yourself is that it allows you to notice, predict, and respond to how others might act. Subjectively, this can feel like being a satellite orbiting your own self. Rather than inhabiting the center of your gravity—like, say, the Earth does—you can feel like the moon rotating around some entity that you are unfamiliar with and have had to shun to survive. That entity is you. The act of shunning yourself feels like the desecration of something sacred. Yet by feeling like you are on the outside looking in on yourself, you are spared feeling the pain of what this survival tactic is doing to your sense of integrity.

> *Kevin recalled a particular moment when this connection to himself was disrupted. At eight years old, he was very strong for his age and loved sports that involved physical contact. One day after school, he played in a backyard football game with some older boys in the neighborhood. He recalled making a lot of tackles and being able to run through their attempts to tackle him. Kevin was met with respect and admiration, an experience that was an accurate reflection of who he actually was.*

> *However, his feelings of personal power, strength, and appropriate aggression were also threatening for him. How could these older boys think so highly of him when his family thought he was so bad? After Kevin arrived home, he looked in the mirror and suddenly had the perception that he was fat. He felt panicked at the thought that he had been fat all this time and nobody had told him. It no longer made sense to him that the older boys had been so impressed by his play in the football game. He was grotesquely fat, so what did that matter?*

> *Kevin carried this (mis)perception through the rest of his adolescence and early adulthood. In therapy, we came to understand it as a Trojan horse designed to put him at odds*

with himself. He felt disgust when he perceived himself, effectively moving him from his own center into becoming an orbiting satellite around himself. Kevin regarded himself the way his mother wanted him to—as putrid and disgusting.

It is important to note here that Kevin did not see himself the way his mother saw him, but rather how his mother wanted him to see himself. Her objective was to disrupt his connection to himself—the good person he was. Kevin had no way to articulate, let alone know, that this profound contempt for his physical appearance did not really come from him. It was only in therapy that he grew to feel safe enough to question this perception and recover his sense of himself as physically strong and powerful.

16

Shaming the Scapegoat for Having Needs

> *Do you fear that if you take offense to someone's behavior, they will say you are too sensitive?*
> *Do you fear that if you say what you want from someone, they will say you are too needy?*
> *Do you work really hard to make it seem like nothing bothers you even when that's not the case?*

The scapegoat survivor often feels like they have less rights than the other person when in close relationship. The narcissistic parent may have sown the seeds of this by trying to embarrass them for asserting their rights in relation to the parent. Narcissistic parents often claim the scapegoat child is "too sensitive" for having legitimate needs. In this chapter, I explain why this so frequently happens in the course of narcissistic abuse.

Why a Narcissistic Abuser Shames the Scapegoat Child for Having Needs

Tiffany was in therapy to recover from growing up as the scapegoat daughter to a narcissistic father. She recalled how he would explode into rages at her for the slightest violation of the household rules. If she waited five minutes before taking the trash out after being asked to, he would attack her character. She would be called disrespectful, inconsiderate, and selfish in a very loud and contemptuous way. Her enabler mother never stepped in to intervene on her behalf.

Tiffany's only frame of reference for understanding her father's behavior toward her was that she must deserve it, yet Tiffany still registered that she felt devastated after his attacks. They seemed to be out of proportion with whatever offense she had supposedly committed. She assumed that her father was reasonable at his core, and so one day she decided she would ask him to speak to her in a calmer tone next time she did something she wasn't supposed to.

"Hey Dad, can I talk with you about something?" she'd asked him. "I was thinking about our fight about the trash last night, and I wondered if it would be possible for you to speak to me in a calmer tone? I know you do not mean it, but it really hurts my feelings when I feel like you're yelling at me."

Her dad looked her in the eye, and a smirk drew across his face as he said, "Damn, Tiffany! You are soooo sensitive! Now, I am not gonna change my behavior just because you're too fragile to take the consequences of your actions."

Tiffany tried to keep her composure after being so cruelly humiliated and was able to mutter "OK" before walking out of the room and finding a private place to cry out the agony she had just endured.

Elements of this example may resonate for many scapegoat survivors. Not every survivor will have sat the parent down like Tiffany did, but you may have known how such a conversation would go for you. This example highlights three reasons why a narcissistic parent will turn the scapegoat child's expression of legitimate needs into something to feel shame about.

Three Reasons a Narcissistic Parent Turns Your Needs Against You

Your Needs Interfere with Their Needs

When you assert your rightful needs to feel respected, this interferes with the narcissistic parent's ability to see you as inadequate. It can also make it harder to use you as a receptacle for their own worthlessness.

Tiffany, for instance, had to work really hard in therapy to challenge her belief that she wasn't good enough. She grew to understand how her father's attacks about the trash were really efforts to make her feel inadequate. Her therapist was able to help her see that they were not based in fact—he attacked because he needed to have someone onto whom he could relocate his own sense of inadequacy.

Tiffany's therapist also helped her understand how her attempt to communicate her legitimate request to be treated with respect threatened her father's ability to keep her as the scapegoat. If he treated her need as legitimate, she might not have been as willing to go along with him the next time he needed to relocate his own worthlessness onto her.

Your Needs Remind Them of What They Do Not Have to Give

The second reason why a narcissistic abuser will turn your legitimate needs against you is that you remind them of what they do not have to give. As a result, the narcissist is put back in touch with their own feelings of inadequacy.

When a scapegoat child goes to the narcissistic parent to ask for what they need, it highlights the lack of compassion the parent feels. If the parent is invested in seeing themselves as compassionate, then they will have to blame the scapegoat child for bringing them into contact with this deficit. Tiffany's father did this by calling her too sensitive, making her request the problem, rather than his own lack of compassion toward her.

Your Needs Remind Them of Their Own Dependency on Others

The third reason why a narcissistic abuser turns your expression of your legitimate needs against you is that they hate their own dependency on others. When the scapegoat child believes it is OK to depend on the narcissistic parent, the parent may be reminded of how they (consciously) forbid themselves to depend on anyone else.

When Tiffany told her father that he hurt her feelings when he spoke to her so harshly, she was also telling him that the way others treat her affects how she feels about herself. This was a statement about her vulnerability—a vulnerability that everyone in touch with their own humanity feels to some extent or another. Her narcissistic father could not stand this need in himself, so instead he went around coercing others to treat him the way he needed to be treated. That is different than what Tiffany was doing. She was not trying to coerce her father to treat her the way she wanted, but appealing to him while granting that it was up to him whether he chose to treat her kindly or not. Granting that others are free to choose to care for the other person or not is what the narcissistic person cannot tolerate. It feels too threatening to them. It did not feel good for Tiffany either in this case, but she was stronger—emotionally and psychologically—than her father, and so could endure the outcome.

The purpose of listing these reasons is to help you understand that there was nothing wrong with what you wanted in these kinds of instances. Rather, you were called too sensitive because what you wanted conflicted with your narcissistic parent's pathology.

17

Gratitude as a Survival Strategy

> *Do you find yourself ready to show appreciation for any act done on your behalf?*
> *Does it feel more natural to worry about whether you have done enough for others than to expect something from them?*
> *Is it foreign to think about how others have failed to meet your needs or expectations?*

Scapegoat survivors often had to cultivate a stance of gratitude toward others regardless of their satisfaction with what was being offered. This stance can be a very important one to adopt in the face of narcissistic abuse. If you survived narcissistic abuse from a parent, you were likely forbidden from showing dissatisfaction with what they were offering you. You may have had to show gratitude for small servings of love, support, or even the absence of harm.

You were likely forbidden from expressing anger at the narcissistic abuser for coming up short in meeting your needs. Doing so would have been met with rebuke, withdrawal, or having your character attacked. When such a condition gets set in a relationship, it ceases to be a relationship in the true sense of the word. It is now a one-way street where the narcissistic parent's needs are all that matter, and it is the child's job to meet those needs and not have his or her own needs or experience get in the way.

In this chapter, I discuss how the scapegoat survivor of narcissistic abuse has to adopt the belief that they are undeserving of getting their needs met by others in order to maintain a stance of gratitude for the small servings offered in a narcissistic relationship. Next, I explain why that grateful stance is a smart one to take to survive narcissistic abuse.

How the Scapegoat Child's Gratitude Is Adaptive

The child who is scapegoated by a narcissistic parent will be perceived as being what the parent cannot stand in themselves. The scapegoat child may be accused of thinking they think they are better than others when it is the narcissistic parent who really thinks this. They may also be accused of being irresponsible (which is just a way of telling the child that he or she is inadequate), again when the narcissistic parent unconsciously fears they are the one who is really inadequate.

Despite directing such mistreatment toward the scapegoat child, the narcissistic parent feels entitled to be treated as superior, special, and exceedingly adequate by them. So what position does this put the scapegoat child in? An emotionally malnourished one, all while being expected to performatively "feed" the narcissistic parent's artificially inflated sense of self.

One very adaptive way to make such a difficult position feel less painful is to believe that you don't deserve much better. If the scapegoat survivor concludes this about themselves, they will no longer feel the anger—and consequent fear of retaliation for expressing this anger—at the narcissistic parent's abuse. Here's how this coping strategy often develops:

When someone does something to anger you, you find reasons why you have no right to be angry. If a friend consistently shows up late to your planned outings, you might censor your angry reaction by saying to yourself, "Well, they have to put up with my (insert bad behavior), so what right do I have to complain?" Or if you are passed up for a promotion at work, you might stem your anger by telling yourself that you could have worked harder this year and should just consider yourself lucky not to be fired.

In the case of a child with a narcissistic parent, it is imperative for that child to find a way to keep the parent willing to care for him or her in whatever capacity is possible. In contrast to adults, children cannot leave the relationship with the parent and survive. Believing themselves to be undeserving in this manner accomplishes a lot for the child in this difficult position:

- It quells the child's anger toward the narcissistic parent, which if expressed would only make things worse for the child
- The child's resulting shows of gratitude for even small displays of decency by the narcissistic parent comply with that parent's elevated sense of self-worth
- The child gets to convince themselves that they have a parent who is worth looking up to at a time in their lives when they absolutely need to believe they have such a person as a parent.

18

Getting Robbed of Self-Worth

> *Does it feel very difficult or even impossible to feel proud of yourself?*
> *Does winning feel like a foreign experience to you?*
> *Do you spend a lot of time trying not to be a disappointment to yourself?*

If you have survived narcissistic abuse by a parent and survived the role of scapegoat, then these questions could very well fit your experience. For the child of a narcissistic abuser, there is no room in the relationship for your strengths, appropriate needs for affirmation and validation, or rightful pride in who you are and what you can do.

In this chapter, I explain how the scapegoat survivor of narcissistic abuse is systematically denied the self-worth medals that they deserve. Next, I describe how the scapegoat child may learn to cope with the narcissistic abuser's withholding of the recognition they need for their positive qualities.

Lack of Recognition

During the Winter Olympics, world-class athletes compete to win medals. Let's take snowboarding as an example. Shaun White is an American athlete who has dominated this event for over a decade. Let's say he has a phenomenal run and then is waiting for the judges to give him his score. Such moments always result in the crowd waiting with bated breath.

I think part of the bated breath moment is our slight anxiety that White will not be justly awarded for his performance—and the hope that he will. And we all breathe a sigh of relief when the judges' score matches our sense of his performance. If the score is lower or higher than this collective sense, there is often an outcry and a feeling that things are not right.

If you were cast into the role of scapegoat by a narcissistic abuser, you could perform like Shaun White in any given domain, yet the score from the abuser would always be way lower than you deserve. You might even be used to being judged as a poor performer by that parent. Perhaps you have learned not to get your hopes up that others' evaluations of you will match the quality of your performance. This can be demoralizing. It can also turn life into a grim affair, because there is no viable path to victory and the resulting pride in yourself.

The scapegoat child can only hope to avoid getting the lowest score possible. That is not a great basis for motivation. No wonder those who have survived scapegoated narcissistic abuse often have trouble motivating themselves to work toward personal and professional goals.

The usual rewards pride, joy, and the thrill of victory—do not feel safe to experience.

How the Scapegoat Is Denied Recognition for Their Efforts

I think the metaphor of the narcissist parent as a corrupt judge at the Olympics is what it is like to grow up as the scapegoat to that parent. The narcissistic parent's core sense of worthlessness, denial of these feelings, insistence that they're instead superior to other people, and mission to "find" their cast-off worthlessness in someone else makes it so that they cannot tolerate giving a good score to the person they've relocated their worthless into.

Unfortunately for the scapegoated child, he or she has no reason to doubt the narcissistic parent's judgments of him or her. Children are born without a frame of reference for who they are in the world and depend on their parents for their very first and often most influential answer. If the parent is narcissistically abusive, the answer that child receives—particularly if that child's natural abilities or qualities threaten the narcissistic parent's fragile sense of superiority—will likely be disappointing or even humiliating.

Here, I think it is really important to distinguish the messages the scapegoat child of a narcissistic parent receives from the essential qualities of that child. Like Shaun White, the child could be excellent in what they do or who they are, and this capability might still evoke a "low score" from the narcissistic parent.

Vanessa was in her thirties and had survived being the scapegoat to a narcissistic mother. In therapy, she tried to make sense of what she'd endured at the hands of her parents.

She grew to recognize some of her very real qualities as a person: she was perceptive, had a keen sense of fairness, was motivated to fight injustices that she encountered, and cared deeply about others' feelings. She recalled being the only one in her family who ever seemed to voice that something felt wrong. At one point, she spoke one-on-one with her father, who had always taken a submissive role to her narcissistically abusive mother and refused to ever intervene on Vanessa's behalf. She asked him, "Did you recognize that I was emotionally the strongest family member?"

Her father immediately cut from his usual passive stance and said gruffly, "I don't know, Vanessa . . . I didn't go around handing out medals!"

As we discussed this moment in therapy, Vanessa immediately felt shame at having supposedly bragged by citing her strength and asking for her father to recognize it. I quickly joined in with, "Well, why didn't he hand out medals? Was that not his job as a father?"

This statement lifted Vanessa's shame, and she could return to her initial rightful question of why her father hadn't given her the medal she deserved for being so strong.

Vanessa's example, and others like it, illustrate how matter-of-factly the scapegoat of the narcissistic family is denied the recognition and pride they deserve in who they are. Vanessa learned to cope with this ongoing denial of the self-worth medals she deserved by not asking for such recognition.

When she was growing up, she didn't have a therapist who could help her work through the humiliating way her family received her very reasonable efforts to be appreciated and recognized for her strengths and capacities. As a kid, she also had no way of knowing that she was up against a psychological pathology in her mother and father that made it impossible for her to get the credit she needed from them. The experience Vanessa had—over and over again—was that when she piped up to ask for someone to witness her gifts or abilities, she experienced shame instead of pride.

When Shame Interferes with Recognition

When someone goes to another person with the intent of sharing something meaningful and vulnerable (like when Vanessa asked her father if he recognized how strong she was), they may expect that person to respond in a validating and supportive way. This might mean communicating that he or she shares the state of mind that the person who is sharing is experiencing. This would've happened if Vanessa's father had said something like, "Boy, did I! I saw it from the moment you were a kid . . . you always had a great bullshit detector and spoke up about it."

When this expectation gets violated, and the other person responds unexpectedly and derisively, it may lead to an intense, burning feeling of shame. So, when Vanessa's father responded dismissively, he was in essence telling her, "You see yourself as deserving encouragement for being so strong, but I see you as weak for needing such recognition in the first place, and I want you to feel embarrassed about that need."

If such experiences happen regularly for the scapegoat child, they may learn to protect themselves by avoiding them altogether.

19

The Power of Language

> *Do you find it difficult to know your own opinion in life?*
> *Do you tend to regard others as the "experts" and defer to their judgment?*
> *Does it seem like whatever you conclude is going to be wrong somehow while others are going to be right?*

If you are familiar with any of these experiences, this chapter may be useful to you. A narcissistic parent's moods and attitudes toward their child can vacillate wildly. If the child happens to be adding to the parent's artificially inflated sense of self-worth, they may be the apple of the parent's eye. Conversely, if the child is trying to exercise their independence in a way that threatens the parent's sense of domination over them, they may be met with scorn and devaluation. For the child, this is incredibly difficult to make sense of on a deep level.

In this chapter, I describe some of the language traps that the scapegoat child of the narcissistic parent may find themselves in. The child struggles to make coherent the fact that the same person they depend on as a frame of reference for what's true says "I love you" one moment, then mistreats them the next. One of the consequences of such contradictory communication is that the child may learn that language doesn't mean that much.

The Importance of Language

I am a big fan of standup comedy, and one of my favorite comics is Nate Bargatze. On his podcast, he and his buddies were discussing language—particularly, the seeming arbitrariness of society deeming some words to be curse words and others not. One of the other guys said something like, "Wouldn't it be nice if we all just decided that no words were bad?" Nate then made the compelling point that if we are going to have words that mean something good—like "I love you"—then we have to have words that mean something bad—like "I hate you." Otherwise, the good words don't mean anything.

I thought this was such a compelling point, and one that children of narcissistic parents often miss out on. When you have a parent whose self-esteem is volatile and who will go to any length to secure a sense of superiority, then what comes out of their mouth can get really confusing. When the parent is feeling good, the child is likely to hear nice things about themselves. Conversely, when the parent is feeling bad, the child is likely to hear a lot of hurtful and cruel things. When a kid desperately wants to believe in the goodness of a narcissistic parent and that parent acts in very contradictory ways, language can get weird for that child.

This happens because the child is hearing something like "I love you" from the same person who has said—and likely will say again—"I hate you." If language is taken seriously, then this scenario does not make sense. I think that the word "love" at its core means something like feeling protected, welcomed, appreciated, accepted, and safe, and getting to feel this way consistently with the same person. The child of a pathologically narcissistic parent knows not to expect such consistency. So if the narcissistic parent says "I love you," but the child feels on edge around that parent and knows that earlier in the day they acted as if they wished the child had never been born, then what happens to the word "love" in the child's mind?

Now the word "love"—and a lot of other language—has been used in ways that betray the child deeply. Language has become a means toward the end of keeping the narcissistic parent pleased instead of being something the child uses to name their experiences and honestly communicate them to others—and to receive honest communications. So, the word "love" is stripped of its meaning as being a feeling of consistent protection and safety with someone and comes to mean "the other person is happy with me at the moment because they feel good about themselves."

Another way that language gets weird during and after narcissistic abuse is in how the child has to use it to excuse the narcissistic parent's cruelty toward them. When the parent is domineering, intrusive, and/or vindictive, the child has to figure out a way to not take prolonged or genuine offense. Often, they can do this by not assigning the correct words to their parent's behavior.

For example, the narcissistic mother may get a look of murderous rage in her eyes and scream at her daughter for leaving her toys out, but the daughter may not say, "Mom is being mean right now." Instead, she may use language to focus on what she herself has supposedly done, rather than applying words to describe her mother in these moments. She might instead say, "I was a terrible daughter for leaving my toys out. I am so bad!" This way, there is no language within the daughter that records the narcissistic mother's bad moments. This can help the daughter deal with the contradiction between her desire to apply the word "love" to a mother who treats her so hatefully at times. Yet, the cost is that the daughter has a sense that language is no longer being used to discover, name, then communicate truth. Its fundamental purpose is getting frayed because of the unsolvable contradictions being presented by the narcissistic parent.

The No-Win Situation

In situations where a narcissistic parent says things or acts in ways that are favorable toward the child, this type of dialogue may occur:

Narcissistic parent: "I love you, child."

Child (to themselves): "My parent hates me and is saying they love me right now. I must be wrong to think they hate me. I am a liar, and they really love me."

OR

Child (to themselves): "My parent hates me and is saying they love me right now. They must be a liar."

Neither of these scenarios work for a child, but it is the first one that must be adopted. The child cannot survive without at least the hope that their parent is there for them. To acknowledge that it is the parent who is misusing language would be to know that the child has no one there for them.

20

Splitting

> *Are your feelings of pain buried far back in yourself,*
> *where nobody can see or hear them?*
> *Do you involuntarily find yourself tuning into what*
> *others' needs more than what you need?*
> *Do you feel a vague fear that never seems to go away?*

Imagine a three year old boy named Matthew who is exquisitely conscious of his smallness and needfulness. At times he feels a continuity of that dependency with someone upon whom he can depend, a bigger person who seems to be there and take delight in the boy. When he's on the swings at the playground, this bigger person pushes him. His belly gets full of tingles, and he laughs uncontrollably. This makes the bigger person laugh too. They share something. Matthew feels like part of an "us."

But sometimes, this bigger person changes. Sometimes, this person is not so friendly. Sometimes, this person gets mad and makes Matthew feel bad. He is not sure what makes the person so mad at him. He is scared. He also misses the good bigger person who was just there. That person seems gone for good, and Matthew is in a world of hurt. But he cannot get near this fear and pain he feels because there is no one to tell about it. Instead, he knows two things about the bigger person at the same time: that 1) he does not want to lose the good bigger person, and 2) he's scared of the bad bigger person and wants to hide from them.

Both are true. How can that be?

This is what attachment trauma can feel like for the scapegoat child of a narcissist. Such children are tasked with knowing two negative things about their parent, and the only way to do this is for the child to dissociate the part of their mind that knows one thing from the part that knows the other thing. This is the "split." It can leave the scapegoat child, and later the adult, in disarray on the inside, as if their center is frayed, and even empty. Good therapy after narcissistic abuse can involve developing a relationship with a good enough therapist who helps you track, know, and eventually feel the feelings that had to be shunned earlier in all their contradictory glory. Therapy that goes on long enough can result in finally feeling safe enough to re-access the feelings that had nowhere to go earlier. This can help you mend the split that often occurs for the scapegoat child.

Where Does Therapy Pick Up for the Scapegoat Survivor of Narcissistic Abuse?

Let's assume Matthew has matured and grown into an adult in his early twenties. He has found a way to manage the feelings evoked and left unresolved by his narcissistic parent, but life has felt full of tension, dis-ease, and vague fear. He lives life more moment-to-moment than having a sense of continuity between himself and others. Although in his head he knows he matters a great deal to his trusted friends and partner, his body has a hard time getting on board with this knowledge. It's like a force of gravity, holding him back from being able to jump high enough to reach a place where he can *feel* their appreciation of him. He feels estranged from his own life. He also feels vibrant, connected to others, and optimistic. Both are true.

Matthew's psyche had to organize around the constant cycle of a seemingly good parent turning against him. It felt beyond catastrophic when as a boy he lost the good bigger person to the bad and scary bigger person. And there was no one to tell. The person he might have told—the bigger person—was the same person who was hurting him. He had to survive this completely on his own. This is the type of trauma that no child's mind is equipped to process.

Nonetheless, Matthew had to go on, and he did. He developed an inner blueprint for what to expect in relationships with others. He grew to expect any good feelings he experienced with others to be temporary. He braced himself for them to lose interest in him, reject him, or recoil from something he did. Sometimes he would feel good with other people, but then he would feel bad. The good did not last, and the bad never went away.

He felt like he was swimming in Loch Ness lake. Sometimes he had to wrestle with the Loch Ness monster. Other times, he could seemingly enjoy the lake and the other swimmers in the water. But even then, the monster still lurked beneath the surface. It just wasn't as visible.

What Can Therapy Do for the Scapegoat Survivor's Split?

Matthew brings all of this duality into therapy. He feels connected to his therapist – Don - in session, while struggling outside therapy to have a firm sense of existence. This gets brought up when Don unexpectedly has to cancel a session at the last minute. Matthew tells him how frustrated and disappointed this makes him. He finds such last-minute cancellations really upsetting, and they're not something he wants to put up with. Don listens to his client's experience. Now Matthew has a new experience. Don is usually like the good bigger person, but when he canceled Matthew was suddenly faced with the bad bigger person again.

This time, however, Don does not attack Matthew but is there to listen. Don wants to know how Matthew felt about having to see the bad bigger person as a result of the session being canceled last minute. It almost seems like Don also doesn't want Matthew to lose the good therapist. This makes losing the good therapist when the cancellation happened feel way less catastrophic than it used to with Matthew's parent.

Don is not always going to be good, but when he is bad, it will be brief, it will be unintentional, and he will be there to hear and care about the impact it has on Matthew. Now Matthew has gotten to experience his therapist as mostly good, sometimes bad, but always *trying* to be good to him, and he begins to experience other people in his life this way too. Eventually, he grows to experience himself in this way. The separateness of the Matthew's experience begins to fade, and things seem to feel more continuous. He feels more real.

It is hard enough for a child with a well-adjusted parent to trust that when that parent fails to be there for the child in the way the child needs, they can still be trusted. The well-meaning parent has to demonstrate accountability, concern for the child's feelings, and an earnest effort to be there the next time. Luckily, kids do not require perfection. So long as the child feels in sync with the parent roughly a third of the time, he or she will have a good shot at healthy development. When a parent acts like the parent of the boy in this chapter, the child faces inner devastation at their failures. Such a child risks losing hope that the parent can or will be there for them the next time. In this story, the man's feelings of irreparable loss were mended in the therapist-client relationship. These ruptures were much briefer, and resolvable in contrast to what he'd experienced with his parent. The man learned that he did not need to resort to dissociation to manage the overwhelming feelings of loss when someone close to him let him down. The split within him could be mended.

Pillar #2:

Gain Distance from the Narcissistic Abuser

21

The Importance of Getting Away from a Narcissistic Abuser

> *Do you feel like you are back in the scapegoat role after any interaction with your narcissistic parent?*
> *Are you left confused over how you can feel so impacted by seemingly "benign" interactions with your family?*
> *Is it hard to know why you feel "less-than" when you are around your narcissistic parent today?*

One of the most challenging aspects in recovering from narcissistic abuse is the task of putting psychological, emotional, and sometimes physical distance between yourself and your narcissistic abuser. Guilt and ambivalence that can emerge when beginning to separate from a narcissistic family. Questions can arise, like: "Am I making all this up?" "Am I being unreasonable?" "Am I being too sensitive?" There can also be something else at play that makes distance feel so challenging to establish—but this "something else" is precisely why distance is so important and beneficial for the survivor.

In this chapter, I discuss the invisible forces that can hold a narcissistically abusive system together. There are some pretty cool ideas in the field of personality research that shed light on these forces. I am going to describe what some of them are and then use them to explain why distance from the narcissistic abuser is so necessary for recovery.

The Forces at Play in a Narcissistically Abusive System

Kurt Lewin, a prominent psychologist in the mid-1900s, researched all the various influences that act on an individual when they are in a certain group context. It is known as "field theory" and does a tremendous job of highlighting how an individual is not a lone operator in any group setting but is responding to all the other people in the environment. He proposed that any single person's behavior in a group is the result of that person's own needs, wishes, goals, desires, and the environmental forces acting upon them. Both the environment and the individual mold and shape each other in their interactions. This happens at both conscious and unconscious levels of experience.

There are three important principles of field theory that apply to narcissistic abuse. The first is that that any action in a family system is both a cause and an effect in the system. Each person acts upon and is acted upon by others. The second principle states that anyone's behavior and experience at a given point in time is the product of the immediate forces acting upon that person at that same point in time. So there is a big emphasis on the present moment. Of course, past patterns have an impact, but current behavior and influence can still be traced to what is happening in the here and now. The third principle is that a system will move toward a state of stability and will resist destabilization. This means that if the individual tries to act in ways that do not contribute to the system's stability, then the system will act in ways to influence the individual to change his actions to be more aligned with the system's stability.

Let's apply Lewin's field theory and these principles to what it can be like for the scapegoat child in a narcissistically abusive family. We'll start with the narcissistically abusive parent, who feels worthless at their core but cannot tolerate this feeling, so they relocate it into the scapegoated child. The narcissistic parent wields a lot of influence over this system because he or she often possesses the most perceived authority in the family. Typically, the narcissistic parent functions in a way where he or she is issuing commands and others are expected to show obedience. The principle of interdependence shows up because the narcissistic parent cannot feel artificially better about themselves if they do not have others to obey their orders. The stability of the family system could very well rest on the narcissistic parent issuing orders and the other family members following those orders.

Many survivors of narcissistic abuse say that they feel this invisible pressure to be as they once were when they are back in contact with their narcissistic family. In a narcissistic family system that achieves stability by accommodating the narcissistic parent's psychopathology, there will be tremendous pressure applied to the scapegoat survivor to get back into the role that contributes to that stability. Survivors can describe this pressure as feeling like a specific form of gravity they experience when back in contact—or even thinking back on—their narcissistic family.

This idea suggests that to be in contact with the narcissistic family as the scapegoat survivor also means being exposed to the forces acting on you to get back into the role. Thus, there you experience pressure to keep the system stable by complying with being devalued. From this point of view, to be back in contact with the narcissistic family poses an extreme danger to the scapegoat survivor.

Understanding the narcissistically abusive family as a field that can envelop the scapegoat survivor can be helpful in understanding why distance is so important. When I emphasize the importance of emotional, psychological, and sometimes physical distance from a narcissistic abuser, it is not to punish the abuser for their wrongs. I think it is just a matter of practicality that in order to recover from chronic narcissistic abuse during childhood, it is necessary for the survivor to remove themselves from the emotional contagion that works to keep them from separating from the family. The scapegoat survivor's beliefs that they are defective and/or undeserving cannot be disconfirmed while operating within this system because too many forces are at work preventing the survivor from doing this—it would be too challenging to the stability of the system.

> *Stephen was a man in his thirties who came to treatment complaining of a pervasive feeling of anxiety in just about everything he did. His therapist quickly diagnosed him as the scapegoat to very narcissistic father and saw his self-criticism and difficulty accessing feelings of pride in himself as adaptations to the narcissistic family he had been born into. His therapist would express her astonishment at the cruelty shown to him and would tacitly encourage him to put distance between himself and his father.*

At first, Stephen had difficulty feeling the same sense of indignation at his treatment that his therapist was showing. He was used to it and still close enough to the field of his narcissistic family that he had difficulty seeing the system's unfairness to him. At the same time, something deep within him seemed to tell him that his therapist was right, and he began to limit the amount of contact he had with his father.

Initially, he and the other family members employed tactics to get Stephen to come back to the family. This involved sending messages that accused him of hurting his father, thinking he was better than them, and questioning his sanity. Stephen worked to pay less and less attention to these messages, eventually deleting them before reading them. The next year was difficult, and he would feel disoriented, empty, profoundly sad, and as though he was doing something very, very wrong. In the meantime, he was slowly but surely finding new fields for himself. He was seeing friends who treated him well more and more often. He was dating with an eye for partners who showed him kindness and stability in themselves. By the end of this year, he could look at his professional and personal achievements and give himself credit for them. This was a feeling and experience that was fairly new to him, as it had been strictly forbidden in the narcissistic family he grew up in.

Stephen's case demonstrates the process and importance of separating from the narcissistic family's field and finding new fields for yourself that nourish and strengthen you.

22

Gaining Distance Versus Avoidance

> *Do you worry that separating from your narcissistic parent means you are not giving them a chance?*
> *Do you fear that you will be avoiding a needed confrontation with your narcissistic parent if you do not explain why you are separating from them?*
> *Are you concerned that you are letting your narcissistic parent get away with mistreating you if you do not confront them?*

Bernard came to therapy in his mid-twenties to find relief from the constant anxiety he experienced in his life. We quickly came to understand that he'd grown up with a narcissistic father who acted in a domineering way around the house and would grow enraged if Bernard responded with anything but obedience. It was no wonder that Bernard grew particularly anxious expressing a difference of opinion at work or in his personal life. At the time, Bernard was attending family dinners at his parents' home every Sunday.

He described how, at these dinners, someone would inevitably do something that displeased his father, who

> would view this as a sign of unforgivable disrespect and proceed to berate, intimidate, and yell at the offender— either Bernard or his mother. In therapy, I inferred that Bernard held the unconscious belief that he did not deserve protection. When we discussed the prospect of limiting his attendance at these dinners given how abusively his father would treat him, Bernard said that he felt like he would be "running away from the problem" if he did this.

Do you have similar concerns when it comes to creating distance between yourself and a narcissistic abuser? In this chapter, I describe how an honest assessment of what is possible with a narcissistic abuser suggests that trying to "confront" the situation will not be productive. Next, I describe the costs to you in trying to confront such individuals. Last, I'll discuss the difference between avoiding an interaction that should be addressed versus protecting yourself from interactions that might only be detrimental to you.

What There Is to Gain

I think it is important to pose this question to oneself whenever we consider addressing a problem in a relationship. Hopefully, most people that you are in a relationship with have the capacity to hear you with an open mind, show concern for your feelings, and prioritize the health of the relationship over being right. And I do not mean to say that every relationship should meet these three criteria every time, but this should be the case more often than not.

When it comes to addressing a narcissistically abusive person with your discontent over how they are treating you, this question is especially important. Consider that a narcissistically abusive person has to elevate their sense of self-worth to feel intact. This elevation consists of seeing themselves as superior, more deserving, and more important than others. They take license to act in a domineering, intrusive, and vindictive fashion to the people in their lives. A narcissistic person is often constantly on watch to see who is not complying with their sense of entitlement to be revered as more important, wiser, and holding more authority.

With all of this in mind, what is to be gained from telling a narcissistic abuser that you are unhappy with their treatment of you? I would argue very little. The most likely outcome is a vindictive attack aimed at undermining the basis for your complaint, your character, and your reputation. As such, confronting the narcissist would endanger your psychological, emotional, and potentially physical safety.

Why Distance from a Narcissistic Abuser Is Self-Care

If you were walking in the woods and came across a rattlesnake sunning itself in the middle of your path, what would you do? Hopefully the answer would be to walk around it to spare yourself any untoward exchange with the creature. Would that be considered avoidance, or an act of self-care? A rattlesnake cannot be talked out of doing the only thing it knows to do to survive what it perceives as a threat—namely, execute its poisonous bite.

Similarly, someone who is pathologically narcissistic cannot be talked out of doing the only thing they know how to do when their inflated sense of self-worth gets threatened—attack, coerce, and devalue the person who is the source of the threat without concern for their feelings. So, if you choose to walk around a rattlesnake or a narcissistic parent, the benefit seems to be ensuring your own survival and not putting yourself in harm's way. That is the essence of self-care.

Guilt: The Sticking Point

When you have survived narcissistic abuse—particularly by a parent—you may experience a strong feeling of responsibility for the narcissist's emotional well-being. You likely assumed this feeling to ensure your survival, because when the narcissistic parent is unhappy, then nobody close to them can be happy either. Therefore, securing their happiness before your own may have been quite necessary. This can also lead to you experiencing your narcissistic parent as fragile and at risk of being destroyed if you do not protect them in this way. Such thoughts and feelings can result in you feeling extremely guilty for taking care of yourself before taking care of them—no matter how unfair you may know this to be.

This guilt takes time and patience to resolve during the process of recovery, and I would encourage you to try to afford yourself compassion as you work toward this. The goal is to notice when you might be taking more responsibility for others' emotional well-being than your own and exercise compassion toward yourself as you consider redrawing the lines of jurisdiction for what you are and are not responsible for.

23

The Journey of the Scapegoat Survivor of Narcissistic Abuse

> *Have you noticed a turning point where you got to question the lack of happiness you had to endure as the scapegoat?*
> *Have you started on the path toward healing yourself from the emotional damage inflicted upon you?*
> *Is it difficult to see yourself as the protagonist in your own life story?*

Being the scapegoat in a narcissistic family is to be saddled with all of the narcissistic parent's problems and sent into psychological and emotional exile. The scapegoat child has to keep finding ways to hold on to the narcissistic parent in the face of this rejection. Usually that's done by believing things that let them perceive the narcissistic parent's abuse as something the child deserves. These are the kinds of beliefs I described in Chapter 10:

"If I am not being productive, then I am worthless."

"I do not deserve protection."

"I am defective."

"I am unattractive."

"I am always one mistake away from complete ruin."

At some point the scapegoat survivor faces a choice of whether to keep living life according to these beliefs or to see if there is a more compassionate and meaningful way to treat themselves.

Scapegoat survivors who are seeking to heal have come to question the ways their narcissistic abuser treated them. They particularly question whether or not they deserved the mistreatment, as the narcissistic abuser claimed. Getting to this point is something that every survivor has to do for themselves. Then the question often becomes—what to do next? In this chapter, I describe the scapegoat's journey in-depth, from being saddled with the burdens of the narcissistic parent's own self-hatred, to questioning whether that hatred belongs to them, to connecting back to a home within themselves that was not safe to occupy when serving as the scapegoat to the narcissistic abuser.

Phase One of the Scapegoat's Journey

The scapegoat child who is in the critical period of developing their sense of identity in the world is at a dramatic disadvantage in fighting against the narcissist's lies. That child needs his family to tell him who he is in the world lest he feel like he is no one to anybody. So, the child finds a way to convince himself that his family is right about how bad he is. Thus, he can now perform the function needed by the narcissistic parent and family—he sees himself as deserving of their sins so that they may live as saints.

In contrast to the origin story of the term scapegoat, so long as the narcissistic family is around, they usually do not cast the scapegoat child into exile, because they need him or her. What typically happens is that the child finds ways to get some distance from the family as they grow up. Whether that takes the form of going on Reddit to read the thread "raisedbynarcissists" or YouTube to find channels on narcissistic abuse, confiding with a friend about what life's like at home, or moving out to go to work or college, the scapegoat child might secure their own exile at one point or another. It is at that point that the scapegoat survivor may find themselves in that emotional rocky headland that the original scapegoat wandered into after being exiled from the village.

Now the scapegoat survivor has the room to entertain a needed existential crisis. In order to play the role of scapegoat to his narcissistic parent, the survivor in essence has had to believe that there is nothing good about him, and that everything is good about the other family members. Yet, as the scapegoat survivor goes about living in the world away from the narcissistic family, he has to do something with the accumulating evidence suggesting that he's not as bad as he's forced himself to believe. He may also wrestle with the growing desire to exist in a way that does not feel so wretched. In these moments, the scapegoat survivor faces a choice: 1) Go on believing he deserves the feeling of sin that he's carried all this time, or 2) Question why he's been burdened with feeling so sinful and start looking for honest answers.

This is the moment I alluded to at the start of this chapter. If you are reading this, you may already have taken this step. Now the question becomes, what's next?

Phase Two of the Scapegoat's Journey

Now the scapegoat survivor is in the rocky headlands of life, saddled with a well-worn sense of who they are that does not serve them anymore. They are familiar with the beliefs that they are defective and undeserving. They are also familiar with the coping strategy of getting away— because the attention they get from others has grown to feel bad rather than good.

In order for the scapegoat to get back to the only home that is truly available to them, they must override this long-practiced coping strategy with a new practice of moving closer to themselves and safe others. This is not done in one fell swoop—or even a few fell swoops. It is a process. And you cannot do this alone.

So, the answer to the question of what's next[4] for the scapegoat survivor who has questioned the edict that he is wretched is: to find and go home. But the catch is that the home resides within himself.

---

[4] Another useful resource to answer this question is my online course on recovery from narcissistic abuse. You can find it here: https://lp.jreidtherapy.com/narcissistic-abuse-course

24

Moving Out of the Narcissistic Parent's Home

> *Did you experience increased hostility and sabotage when you left—or attempted to leave—your narcissistic parent's home?*
>
> *Were you fearful that your narcissistic parent would find a way to prevent you from leaving?*
>
> *Are you still living with your narcissistic parent and wary of what they will do if you move out?*

Rick grew up as the scapegoat in a family dominated by a narcissistic mother. He was roundly criticized and yelled at on a daily basis for not doing chores around the house in a "responsible enough" way, not showing enough deference to his mother, and wanting to see friends outside the family.

By the end of high school, Rick had had to winnow his life down to working extremely hard in school and doing his chores around the house. He harbored the secret wish to escape the torment of his home by going to college. Around May of his senior year, he was accepted, and began to make plans to live a life that felt less like prison. He was in a for a terrible surprise. From the day he got into college until the end of the summer when he left, his mother ratcheted up her attacks to an almost unbearable degree. Rick found himself developing even more intense self-criticism when he was alone with his thoughts. By the time he got to school, he was so ridden with anxiety over not passing his courses, not finding friends, and being a failure that he found it almost impossible to concentrate and do what would have otherwise come naturally to him.

Did you have an experience similar to Rick's when it came time to leave the home of your narcissistic parent? If so, then I hope you will find this chapter useful. One of the most hopeful yet psychologically and emotionally dangerous times for the scapegoat child of the narcissistic parent is when it is time to move out. Whether it is to leave for college, the armed forces, or a job and your own place to stay, these moments signify an act of independence by the scapegoat child that may prove threatening to the narcissistic parent. In this chapter, I dig into the psychological necessity for the narcissistic parent to feel dominant and in control of the scapegoat child. Next, I explain how the narcissistic parent acts coercively to enforce the scapegoat child's submission to their efforts at control. Third, I address the psychological and emotional dangers often faced by the scapegoat child or adolescent when they move out. Last, I will offer a strategy that can be used to protect yourself when moving out from under a narcissistic parent's control.

The Narcissistic Parent's Psychological Need to Dominate the Scapegoat Child

A narcissistic parent has forged a solution to the problem of a deep sense of worthlessness that is hurtful to others. They have denied these feelings, insisted on their opposite (that they are in fact worth more than others), and feel entitled to coercively use others to support their fashioned superiority. Their artificially inflated self-worth is a fragile one and offers only temporary relief from the latent worthlessness, powerlessness, and shame they are constantly trying to elude. However, the cost to those close to them is that they are forced to collude with the narcissist's efforts to prop themselves up. Any action from another person which does not do this will result in break-through feelings of worthlessness for the narcissist, who will typically attack the other person for failing to prop them up.

I remember a rhyme kids used to say when I was in first grade: "I'm the boss, you're applesauce / Understand, rubber band?"

Not exactly contemporary hip-hop, but it always stuck with me, and I think perfectly encapsulates the narcissistic parent's attitude toward the scapegoat child. In order for that parent to feel superior, they need to feel like the boss of you. Regarding you as being "applesauce" I think reflects how the parent implicitly devalues the child to assume the position of boss. Same goes with calling the other a "rubber band." It is playful in the rhyme but really gets at the heart of the narcissist's need to domineer others.

How the Narcissistic Parent Coerces the Scapegoat Child to Submit to Their Control

The narcissistic parent perceives the scapegoat child to be a psychological extension of themselves. Just as we move our fingers if we so choose, the narcissistic parent can believe it is the child's inherent duty to obey the parent's command in the same way. Any hesitation or outward protest at being told what to do will likely be experienced as outrageous, a sign of being ungrateful, and a betrayal. Therefore, any effort by the scapegoat child to take control of themselves rather than bending to the will of the narcissist will be grounds for punitive attack. Narcissistic rage, systematic efforts to undermine the child's good standing to others in and outside the family, and overt rejection can all happen to the scapegoat child who dares to live based on the dictates of their own will rather than the narcissistic parent's will.

The Dangers of Moving Out for the Scapegoat Adolescent

Given how necessary it is for the narcissistic parent to be in charge of the scapegoat child, it's no surprise that it can be extremely dangerous for that child to leave the home. The scapegoat moving out may bring the narcissistic parent face-to-face with their inability to control the child. As the narcissist typically tries to devalue those whom they cannot control, this may happen intensely in the lead-up to the departure of the scapegoat child from the home—just as it did for Rick in the example at the start of this chapter.

It is an act of great courage for the scapegoat adolescent to move out in the face of such malevolence from the narcissistic parent. I wrote this chapter to hopefully inform adolescents who are currently in this situation or adults who see an adolescent who is in this situation to be aware of the dangers of the narcissistic parent's increased attacks when the child is planning to leave home. My hope is that this awareness may help such children to identify how the parent is acting, why they are doing this, and how the child might protect themselves from believing the malicious attacks being wielded against them.

The scapegoat leaving flies in the face of the narcissistic abuser's requirement to feel in control of the victim and can inspire murderous levels of narcissistic rage to restore this sense of control.

How to Protect Yourself When Moving Out

I think that the most important tactic when leaving the home of a narcissistically abusive parent is to find connections to safe others whom you can confide in and feel support from. It will be very important to experience others feeling happy with you exercising your independence to counter your narcissistic parent's accusations that you are defective for wanting to leave. In addition, if you are worried about your physical safety as you transition out of the narcissistic parent's home, these other people may be able to offer you protection. In short, the narcissistic abuser preys on the scapegoat child's isolation from others so that only the parent has a say in how the child feels about himself or herself. If you are in this position and can find alternative sources of self-worth in other good relationships, the narcissistic parent will lose a great deal of power over you.

25

What to Do after Creating Distance from a Narcissistic Abuser

> *Do you feel a nagging sense of unfinished business with your narcissistic parent?*
> *Is it hard to know what to do with the emotional space created after separating from a narcissistic parent?*
> *Do you feel a strong impulse to "set the record straight" with your narcissistic parent?*

One of the people who purchased my online course for recovery from narcissistic abuse wrote a post that raises an important question in the accompanying private Facebook group for those enrolled in the course. They gave me permission to quote them directly here.

> *Every time I watch a video of yours or well, breathe... I want to angrily point out to my dad and mom, "Look! This is you!!!! This is how you hurt me!"*
>
> *I've created distance and plan to only see them on certain occasions. But my dad keeps poking me with vague and empty texts randomly once every couple of weeks that say,*

> "Hope you are having a nice day, love Dad." I have not replied because I feel like he just wants to draw me back in. They both act like all is well.
>
> I am angry. I want them to understand. I do not want it to be a hushed, "Oh, my daughter is going through something", " She's acting strange." I want to scream at them that they hurt me and how and that I am done.
>
> But everything I've read and the Facebook community from the course says, "Just let it go. No good comes of it. They'll never understand."

This person—we'll call her Serena—points to some important issues that this kind of distancing may raise. What about the absence and aggravation that's often left in the wake of putting distance between yourself and a narcissistic abuser? What about the impossibility of getting that person to recognize the damage they have inflicted upon you? What about restitution? These are all important questions that deserve answers. In this chapter, I'm going to talk about the challenge that Serena so aptly describes, then offer a strategy for filling the void left by the narcissistic abuser's absence.

Lack of Closure with the Narcissistic Abuser

An important source of motivation for recovering from narcissistic abuse can be a growing sense of deservingness and corresponding outrage at being treated in such an undeserving way by someone who is pathologically narcissistic. I think this reaction is necessary to begin questioning the ways you are being put down or ignored by the narcissistic person.

For example, let's imagine that Serena's father was narcissistic and held an indifferent and derisive attitude toward her. She had to accept this as normal for most of her upbringing, and learned to expect mockery if she reported an accomplishment. If she said, "I won the spelling bee at school," at dinner, her father would have said something like, "You must have been able to spell 'cat' better than your classmates." As he snickered, Serena's mother would have chortled along with him.

These types of insults numbered in the thousands by the time Serena was ready to graduate high school and move out. She began to examine herself apart from her parents and question why she felt she held such a low status in her family, yet people outside her home regarded her with respect and even admiration. Over time, this led her to stop questioning these other people's positive perceptions of her and begin questioning her parents' reactions. Of course, it took a lot of work and support for Serena to come to this conclusion. As this process of healing continued, she grew more and more indignant at the ways her parents had ignored her and put her down for so much of her life. It had been easier to stomach when she felt she didn't deserve better, but now that she felt more deserving, their treatment of her felt repugnant, and she wanted them to see this.

This is a completely imagined scenario, but it illustrates how strong the pull can feel to set things straight with a narcissistic abuser. So, what sorts of tactics might Serena use to best promote her continued recovery from her father's narcissistic abuse?

Filling the Vacuum Left by the Narcissist

Unfortunately, someone who is pathologically narcissistic and not in treatment themselves is unlikely to be capable of offering a response that is healing to the survivor. In the scenario above, Serena's father unconsciously relocated his own sense of worthlessness into Serena and used denial to entertain any other possibility in order to protect his own fragile yet inflated sense of self-worth.

If a scapegoat child tries to distance themselves from their narcissistic parent, I think a probable response from someone like Serena's father might be what she alluded to in her comment. He might express indifference to her directly, then go around to other people exclaiming that there something is "wrong" with his daughter, and he's not sure that she's OK mentally. This would amount to a smear campaign in whispered tones.

In short, such a confrontation would likely feel like a boomerang turning back on Serena and not be helpful to her process of recovery. So what should she do about her feelings of unease and lack of closure if she is not able to set the record straight with her parents?

Someone once said that nature abhors a vacuum. If there is an absence somewhere, it tends to get filled. In Serena's case, the absence is the lack of her parents' presence in her life, and we might say it is getting filled by the understandable desire to have her grievance addressed by them.

One strategy that Serena is already using is to lean in to the relationships and resources that readily offer her validation and support.

This is a different—and ultimately more healing—way to fill the vacuum. I am suggesting that you move toward such relationships in the aftermath of getting distance from a narcissistic abuser. This can help you accrue more and more experiences of feeling like you matter, like your perspective has value, and that you deserve respect.

As this happens over time, it can often feel less and less galling that your narcissistic family treated you the way they did. This is not because you believe that you deserved that mistreatment, but because at some point, their opinion of you will just stop mattering. In a lot of ways, that will afford you the power that might be part of what you seek in looking for closure with the narcissist. That is, the narcissist got you into a tug-of-war when they were a grown adult and you were a child, so of course they were going to win.

If you try to play tug-of-war now, they are going to claim that they are still winning even if you clearly pull them to your side. One of the worst parts of all of this is the powerlessness you may feel in recognizing your "victory." But when you effectively drop the rope and walk away without looking back to see the narcissist's reaction, you may find a new sense of power. This is the power of self-definition, where it is your own opinion—and that of those who are readily supportive of you—that matters most.

26

Safety First: The Secret to Processing Narcissistic Abuse Trauma

> *In your mind, do you try to go over the bouts of abuse you suffered from your narcissistic parent in hopes of an emotional release?*
>
> *Do you assume that you will have to feel worse before you can feel better in recovery from narcissistic abuse?*
>
> *Do you spend so much time thinking about or researching narcissism that it interferes with your other daily activities?*

I think there is an idea in the world of recovery from any sort of trauma—narcissistic abuse included—that it requires revisiting the feelings that were felt during the abuse, and that if those feelings are felt and those experiences re-examined properly, the survivor will be released from it all. Although that may sometimes work, I have found that in a lot of cases, there is a different path toward healing that operates based on a very different principle.

Jermain came to treatment in his twenties and said he wanted help feeling more confident in his role as a manager at a home construction company, to feel happier in his relationship with his girlfriend, and to pursue hobbies that would bring him happiness and purpose.

Jermain had survived an upbringing in a very narcissistically abusive family, where he faced daily emotional and physical abuse. He'd learned to soothe himself by drinking alcohol in his teens and early twenties and was still susceptible to periodic binge drinking episodes when he felt stressed. In therapy, he started working under the assumption that he needed to talk in-depth about the ways his narcissistically abusive father had demeaned, intimidated, and dehumanized him. Jermain would get a faraway look in his eyes when he went into these details and reported wanting to have a drink after such sessions.

In his third session, as Jermain started to go into a detailed recounting of a time his father had thrown him down their stairwell, his therapist said, "Hey Jermain, where would you say you are right now, from zero to ten, in terms of your stress level?" Jermain answered, "Probably a 7."

His therapist looked at him. "Right, that was my sense ... You're describing something really upsetting that you survived, and our goal here is for you to eventually know what happened, but in a way that makes it clear to you and your nervous system that you are safe now. My concern is that we have not done enough work on shoring up your sense of safety in your life today to productively examine what you went through."

"Well, what do you mean?" Jermain asked. "That I should talk about other things in my life rather than all the messed-up stuff they put me through? Is not the point that we go over these things so that they stop affecting me so much?"

His therapist said, "Well, sort of, but our systems are very wise when it comes to healing from the kind of trauma you went through, and when we take care of our nervous systems and nourish ourselves in the present, then the knowledge we need to put the past to rest usually spontaneously happens. So, what if we did some breathing exercises to get you down to a three or a four on the scale? And I'd like for you to tell me if at any point you get above a four in today's session, so we can stop and do some breathing that'll return you to a lower level. I invite you to use the time in therapy to talk about the goals you mentioned at the start of our work. I remember you wanted to feel more confident at work, happier in your relationship, and to pursue interests that brought you satisfaction."

Jermain was shocked that talking about what was important to him right now was OK to do in therapy, but he started discussing what got in the way of him feeling more confident in his managerial abilities. This led to him understanding how he'd had to downplay his abilities to avoid attack in his family, and he grew to consider that it might now be safe for him to give himself credit.

Jermain's focus on what he wanted for himself in the present, and using therapy to help him move through the obstacles in his way, led to him feeling much stronger and safer in his current life. After a few months of working this way in therapy, he said, "You know, it's strange, but I have a different relationship to what happened to me back then. Somehow, living my life in the ways we've discussed here lets me see how wrong and cruel my family were for doing what they did to me. But I don't think I could've felt this way if I hadn't first embraced my strengths like we've done here . . . "

A spontaneous feeling of tears washed over him. "Wow, these feelings are different . . . They're helping me heal, they're not keeping me stuck." His therapist said, "You've done the work needed to know that it is now safe for you to feel the compassion and sorrow for yourself. We often need to first get to safety before it is possible to experience such feelings."

I bring up Jermain's case to illustrate how important it can be to first build a sense of safety in your current life before looking to process the trauma you have survived. This can especially apply to scapegoat survivors of narcissistic abuse. In this chapter, I explain why it is so important to find safety—and take appropriate measures to build that safety—if you find that trying to re-examine past narcissistic abuse is leaving you stuck instead of feeling more healed.

Do You Have to Feel Worse before You Can Feel Better?

In movies and TV shows, we often see therapy depicted as a process where a client revisits buried feelings that need to be experienced, and once this happens, he is freed from the suffering that his denial of those feelings was causing him. For some clients, the idea that one must feel worse before it is possible to feel better may be a great map for the process of therapy. But for others—including some survivors of narcissistic abuse—a different sequence for healing can apply.

In these cases, it is often first necessary to feel better before you can safely feel worse. Jermain's case is a great example of this. His family used him as the scapegoat and blamed him for their problems while undermining his ability to solve the problems he was being blamed for. For instance, at family dinners, his father would typically find reason to criticize Jermain—often for putting his elbows on the dining table, even if briefly. He would launch into a tirade about how disrespectful and immature Jermain was, saying he wasn't going to stop getting on his case until he learned to have good table manners "like the rest of the family." Jermain would feel like he could not win in these circumstances. He unconsciously knew that if he did not put his elbows on the table, his father would find some other excuse to attack him. This left Jermain feeling like he couldn't do anything right in his life.

For people who have survived the kind of treatment Jermain did, the process of closely examining this type of abuse may be less preferable to shoring up your sense that you can, in fact, do a lot of things right in the world. Here's why: When we suffer a trauma like narcissistic abuse, the only thing to do when it is happening is to survive it. At the same time, such traumatic experiences tend to get encoded in a vivid and fixed way in our minds. When we go back to these memories, there is often this fixedness that can happen, where all we are aware of is the event playing in our mind. It can be very difficult to stay connected to yourself in the present, and as a result, it can be even harder to know that you have in fact survived the abuse and that now growth is possible. Instead, it can result in a reinforcement of that fixation on what happened, coupled with the vividness that often accompanies such memories.

Jermain found the tactic of first acting—in and out of therapy—as if growth was possible for him much more helpful. Then, and only then, could he regard what his family put him through from a vantage point that allowed him to know he had already survived and escaped it, which let him feel his grief at having been through this.

I think it is important not to regard the focus on matters in your day-to-day life as not "dealing with the trauma." For Jerome, by shifting his attention to what was important to him today, he was escaping the fixation of attention that can so often happen after trauma. I would also argue that his focus on what he wanted in his current life implicitly challenged his narcissistic father's rule that he did not deserve anything good because he was supposedly defective. For someone like Jermain, the notion that he must first process trauma before he can live his life could risk reinforcing his father's message that there is something wrong with him, and that he therefore does not deserve the same rights as everyone else.

This notion of "safety first" is not just a shot from the hip. It is actually the basis for the type of therapy I practice, called control-mastery theory. In this theory, the idea is that clients must first experience a specific sense of emotional safety in the therapeutic relationship before they can achieve insight into the traumas they have survived. The argument is that clients are independently motivated to find such safety in the treatment so that they can achieve the growth they desire.

Jermain did this when he told his therapist his three goals at the start of treatment. His therapist picked up on this and showed flexibility in reorienting the therapy around these goals, which likely sent the message to Jermain that it was safe to treat himself like he was a whole and intact person, and deserving of going after what he wanted. Once he felt safe in doing this, he could safely look at how undeservedly cruel his narcissistic father had been to him. So, this approach to healing from narcissistic abuse involves feeling good before safely feeling worse in order to heal.

27

Moving toward Safe People

> *Do you know the importance of finding safe people but don't know how to find them?*
> *Is it extremely unfamiliar to you to feel safe with another person?*
> *Do you worry that you can't trust your feelings when they signal whether someone else is safe or not?*

In this chapter, I emphasize the importance of finding and building relationships with safe people. This is the crux of recovery from narcissistic abuse. The scapegoat child was hurt when their narcissistic parent responded with scorn, contempt, or disinterest at the child's expressions of their true self. In recovery, the goal is for the survivor to express themselves again to a safe person and be received with appreciation, support, and love. In simple terms, the scapegoat survivor learned that being themselves in relationship to others hurts. The goal is to get close to different people today, where being yourself in relationship to them feels good.

So how do you identify safe people? This chapter is designed to help you answer this question for yourself. I encourage you to revisit it as you move through the three pillars of recovery to orient yourself to these principles as needed.

After suffering narcissistic abuse, it can be difficult to know what you can expect from relationships with others. The scapegoat child's mission was to survive chronic mistreatment by the narcissistic family. The child may never have had the chance to ask themselves what qualities they did and didn't want in a friend or partner. It can understandably be hard for a scapegoat survivor to expect something from a relationship that they have never experienced firsthand.

Whether you have prior experience with being treated well or not, this chapter can show you what *should be* possible in relationships. You can then use your emotional imagination to assess which of these possibilities you want and which you do not. As you can see, identifying safe people involves paying attention to your own reactions and feelings. This shift in attention itself can be unfamiliar to the scapegoat survivor. As a child, paying more attention to your own experience over the narcissistic parent's was likely forbidden.

I suggest that, if you are able to create enough psychological, emotional, and/or physical distance from your narcissistic abuser, it may now be possible to pay attention to yourself in this way. And take heart, because when you populate your life with safe people, they will expect and encourage you to pay attention and listen to yourself. In fact, being connected to oneself is something that strengthens safe relationships rather than threatens them.

How to Find Safe People and Move Away from Unsafe People

Once you have identified people who you believe are safe in your life today, it may still feel scary to approach them. After all, the scapegoat survivor's repeated experience in trying to be close to others has usually been rejection. You may have coped by adopting the belief that you were undeserving of others' acceptance. As a result, you may find yourself predicting rejection even when approaching a presumably safe person. Such predictions usually lead us to feel endangered, which may make us retreat from the source of the danger.

It can be important to challenge these feelings of danger that stem from predicting rejection. The chapters in the section about the first pillar of recovery—Making Sense of What Happened—are all designed to give you insight into the falsity of the messages sent to you about your lovability by the narcissistic parent. Your narcissistic parent's rejection of you certainly would have felt personal. However, their behavior was a reflection of how much they hated themselves and the pathological way they had of managing their self-hatred.

A Sample Checklist of Who's Safe and Who's Not

It may be helpful to see a sample checklist of what makes someone safe versus unsafe. I compiled this list based on my own definition of this, and I encourage you to pull from it what you find helpful and add whatever qualities are important to you.

A safe person:

- Seeks to get to know me
- Makes themselves available for me to know
- Shares their struggles with me
- Makes me feel comfortable sharing my struggles
- Makes room for me to share myself
- Shows curiosity about me
- Shows appreciation for me
- Seeks to understand with empathy before judging
- Is slow to anger
- Is capable of resolving a rupture in the friendship/relationship
- Is accepting
- Exercises discretion and protects my confidentiality (does not talk about people behind their backs)
- Makes it clear that they need and want my friendship as much as I need and want theirs
- Is consistent
- Maintains appropriate boundaries in the relationship
- Is respectful
- Has my back

The Challenge of Moving Away from Unsafe People for Scapegoat Survivors

There are objective ways that people can be safe versus unsafe—it is not just subjective. Scapegoat survivors can learn to trust their inner experience as a guide toward safe people and away from unsafe people.

One of the harms of narcissistic abuse is the lack of validation of the fact that how the narcissistic parent is treating you is unsafe. As a child, you may have felt inadequate, fearful, intimidated, and bullied around the narcissistic parent. These are all signs of an unsafe person. Yet the child of such a parent needs stay close to them. It may have been necessary for you to distrust your own felt reactions to others. Such distrust may manifest in thoughts like, "I'm too sensitive," "I'm prone to feeling abandoned because of my history," "I'm too needy," "I'm too much for people to take sometimes," and so on. Doubt your true reactions to others in these ways would have been helpful in staying connected to the narcissistic parent.

In recovery from such abuse, you get to practice taking your reactions to others seriously. You will be encouraged to ask, "Why am I left feeling this way in relation to this specific person?" If you feel like your needs are not being met in a relationship, then what are the specific actions or lack of actions on the part of the other that are contributing to this feeling? Examine these things rather than assuming it is just your fault or flaw.

You get to place accountability on the other person rather than blame yourself when relationships do not feel good to you. You can take an inventory of how your felt reaction matches your assessment of the other person. Now you have a wealth of data upon which to base your decision of whether this person is safe to you or not.

The Challenge of Moving toward Safe People for Scapegoat Survivors

So, you have identified who feels unsafe to you in your life today. For scapegoat survivors, the next step of moving away from such people is its own accomplishment in recovery. In order to survive your parent's narcissistic abuse, you likely had to adopt beliefs designed to keep you in relationship to this unsafe parent. You needed the parent too much for survival to do otherwise.

As a result, moving away from an unsafe person today can mean defying a rule for living that has been around for you for a long time. Defying such rules can often lead to guilt, self-doubt, and even self-condemnation. All of these reactions are founded on two principles: 1) that you are responsible for the other person's emotional well-being, and that 2) the other person's needs are more important than your own.

Chapter 30 (How to Overcome Guilt after Leaving a Narcissistic Abuser) can be helpful in learning to challenge the first principle. In addition, all of the chapters in the section on the third pillar of recovery—Defying the Narcissist's Rules—can be helpful in challenging the second principle. The videos and private Facebook group in my online course[5] is another resource. The videos go into further depth on explaining the pull to prioritize and meet others' needs. The Facebook group offers support and reinforcement from other survivors in your efforts to re-align your own needs as important in your life.

---

[5] You can find it here: https://lp.jreidtherapy.com/narcissistic-abuse-course

28

Breaking Free of the Trauma Bonds of Narcissistic Abuse

> *Do you fear that if you listen to what you're unhappy about in a relationship, it will be impossible to be happy with anyone?*
>
> *Do you fear a terrible retribution, comeuppance, or profound humiliation if you dare to move away from a friend or partner who is treating you poorly?*
>
> *Does it seem like having someone there is a lot more important than expecting them to treat you the way you want to be treated?*

If you grew up with a narcissistic parent and no other viable adult to attach to, it may have been necessary to forge a trauma bond to that narcissistic parent in order to survive. In this chapter, I am going to focus on what a trauma bond is, how it is different from an attachment bond, how a trauma bond can make it hard to create distance from a narcissistic abuser, and finally, offer a tactic to help you operate out from under the influence of the trauma bond's guidance.

Trauma Bonds between the Scapegoat Survivor and the Narcissistically Abusive Parent

As I've stated, a narcissistically abusive person feels a deep and often unconscious sense of worthlessness that they cannot tolerate and cope by insisting on the opposite: that they are worth more than others. Then they expect and influence others to reflect back this inflated view of their self-worth. Last, they lack empathy for the feelings of others, as this would get in the way of being able to seamlessly use others to prop up their inflated self-esteem. As such, being in relationship to such a person is really a one-sided affair.

Now imagine the experience of a child born to such a parent in a context where the other parent does not afford that child much of a different option. The child's own inner world will not matter to the narcissistically abusive parent. They may have ideas about how they want to feel around the child, and if the child gratifies the parent, a type of harmony may occur. However, if the child frustrates the narcissistic parent, they may punish the child in one of two ways: 1) actively hurt the child, or 2) withdraw from the child. In short, the parent can threaten the child with annihilation or abandonment if the child does not make the narcissistic parent feel the way they want to feel. This is the "trauma" in trauma bond for the child of a narcissistically abusive parent.

Now let's contrast this with what an attachment bond looks like for a child born to a good-enough or non-narcissistic parent. For this child, the parent has a non-possessive curiosity, compassion for, and desire to facilitate the growth of the child's mind and developmental strivings. The parent is happy when the child is happy with him or herself. There is an implicit separation between the parent and the child's mind, and the parent maintains and respects this boundary. This parent also manages their own emotional well-being fairly well and is therefore available to the child as a resource to help the child manage his or her own. You will notice that the child does not face any sort of threat of annihilation nor abandonment in any of this. Of course there are moments of frustration for the child in relationship to the good-enough parent, but these are infrequent and tend to be repaired.

Trauma Bonds versus Attachment Bonds

A trauma bond is forged with a frightening and/or frightened parent while an attachment bond happens with a stable and loving parent. Joseph Schwartz describes how attachment bonds develop slowly and are based on mutuality and care (2015). Trauma bonds happen instantly and are based in domination and terror.

To the child, both types of bonds feel essential for survival. A child with an attachment bond to a parent will feel soothed and well-regulated when near that parent. A child with a trauma bond to a parent will feel a confusing mix endangerment, relief, and tension. The child with an attachment bond will feel separate yet connected to their parent. The child with a trauma bond fears being separate from the parent because of the punishment they could face. The child with an attachment bond feels free to make their own decisions. The child with a trauma bond must obey the decisions of the parent.

Trauma Bonds in Movies: *Gone Baby Gone*

The movie *Gone Baby Gone* does a great job of illustrating the difference between an attachment bond and a trauma bond. In it, Casey Affleck and Bridget Moynahan play neighborhood detectives who are helping a police detective solve the case of a missing girl who has been kidnapped. Her mother is known to use and traffic drugs, and the movie makes it clear that she routinely neglects and endangers her daughter.

I do not want to be too much of a spoiler here, but in the end, the kidnapping turns out to have been jointly orchestrated by the chief of police and the detective. The police chief and his wife, who could offer the child a loving and safe upbringing, intended to raise her themselves. This places Casey Affleck's character, who is steeped in the Catholic church and has a real "honor thy parents" outlook, in a moral dilemma. Does he return the girl to her biological mother, or let her continue living with the police chief's family, where she seems very happy?

In *Gone Baby Gone*, this choice is between returning the kidnapped girl to a parent with whom she may share a trauma bond, or let her stay with people whom she seems to be developing an attachment bond to.

For a person who is forced to forge a trauma bond to a narcissistically abusive parent, it is imperative that they to learn to ignore themselves. No one else is benignly paying attention to them, and paying attention to themselves and expecting the same from others only results in one of the two traumas: annihilation or abandonment. The resulting feelings can seem unsurvivable to the child, so it is adaptive to find a way to pay less attention to themselves. In fact, the child who had to forge a trauma bond to a narcissistic parent may even find it difficult to recognize his or her self in the world. Life can feel passable, so long as they are not aware of themselves. Furthermore, being aware of themselves can interfere with doing what's necessary to maintain the trauma bond to the narcissistically abusive parent.

This is why being traumatically bonded to a narcissistic abuser can make gaining distance so difficult for the survivor. The premise of recovery from this kind of abuse involves paying attention to yourself, yet this act can feel like inviting the very traumas you have been having to avoid all your life. You may have had to keep your focus on what is going on around you—at all costs—in order to stave off the anxiety or even terror that would otherwise have flooded in.

The warning signals from the lessons of the trauma bond that can flash include feeling completely unjustified in considering separating from the narcissistically abusive parent or family, wondering if you're making all of it up, etc. Another common fear at this point is that if you pay attention to yourself and what you like versus do not like in relationships, you will never find someone whom you're satisfied with. This concern can seem very reasonable, yet directly mirrors the dilemma you faced earlier in life: if you had decided you were not happy with your narcissistically abusive parent, then you would have been left with no one to attach to.

I don't think these concerns are necessarily what they seem at face value but rather serve the function of keeping the survivor in the only kind of bond they have ever known—the trauma bond to the narcissistic abuser. Additionally, they lead you to not do the thing—pay attention to yourself—that would have gotten you either destroyed or left before.

Strategies to Break the Trauma Bond

Schwartz points out that an attachment bond is built slowly, while a trauma bond develops instantly. That's useful to frame what I am about to say, because this is a process that requires compassion and patience toward oneself—even when such compassion and patience does not feel available.

One way to gradually and compassionately help yourself out of the trauma bond is to set an intention to pay attention to yourself throughout your days. Activities like mindful meditation or connecting to your bodily experience via a daily yoga practice can be very helpful in this regard. Engaging in these activities puts you in the center of your attention.

29

The Scapegoat's Instinct to Include Others

> *Do you reflexively put others' needs ahead of your own?*
> *Does it feel immoral to say what or who you do not like?*
> *Do you feel responsible for the feelings of others?*

In my work with individuals who have survived being the scapegoat in their narcissistic family of origin, I am almost always struck by their deep capacity to understand, empathize with, and offer acceptance to the experience of other people. It is striking, because these people exhibit these instincts despite (for the most part) not having experienced this treatment firsthand in the homes they grew up in. It is like the option to reject, judge, condemn, or put down has never seemed viable to them. In this chapter, I will offer an understanding that hopefully celebrates this attribute of many scapegoat survivors while explaining how it can sometimes get in the way of creating needed distance from one's narcissistically abusive family. Next, I will offer a strategy to help you challenge the notion that creating boundaries for yourself means excluding others who deserve your inclusion.

Why the Scapegoat Survivor Feels Inclusive of Others

The scapegoat survivor knows firsthand how painful it feels to be singled out and rejected by a group that you just want to belong to—your own family. It makes no sense to the person when it is happening. If that group is their only hope of belonging to anyone, then the scapegoated person has to find a way not to blame the group, but themselves, for their rejection. All the while, many scapegoats have an exquisite inner record of how painful this entire ordeal is for them. But why would this lead to wanting to protect others from feeling this way?

I think that by virtue of knowing their own feelings so well, it becomes easy for the scapegoat child to feel empathy toward others who might feel similarly. In addition—and this is anecdotal, not based on research findings that I can cite—scapegoat survivors may be endowed with a higher genetic capacity for empathy. My argument here is that scapegoat survivors may be operating on a natural endowment for compassion and emotional connection to the feelings of others.

The scapegoat's higher than average amount of empathy can predispose the them toward feeling inclusive of others. The scapegoat child was often forbidden from saying what they didn't like about the narcissistic parent. It may have been a matter of survival to show continued appreciation toward the parent regardless of the scapegoat child's true preferences or opinions. Given the limited available options for sources of self-worth in the narcissistic family, the scapegoat may thus have derived pride from their willingness to see the good in everyone else and respond to them in kind.

As a result, you as the scapegoat may feel like a bad or worthless person if you entertain negative thoughts or feelings about others. It may feel like you're losing the one thing that makes you special and worthwhile.

The Challenge of Being Inclusive When It Comes to Recovery

As adaptive a trait as inclusiveness is for the scapegoat survivor, this practice can interfere with the second pillar of recovery: gaining distance from the narcissistic abuser. It is an important milestone when the scapegoat survivor grows to feel safe in exercising discretion over whom they do and do not offer inclusiveness to. This is an important step toward recovery, because they have previously had to act inclusively toward someone who was rejecting toward them. By keeping this person close, the scapegoat has had to compromise their own self-care. I believe that it takes repeated experience in new, safe relationships to post-traumatically learn that you can exercise discretion without losing the people you need most in life. Importantly, this was not the case in the past, but with the right people, it is now a possibility.

Choosing to create and maintain distance from a narcissistic abuser may require some compassionate self-talk when feelings of guilt or self-blame emerge. You can reframe the right to exclude people who mistreat you as a non-injurious act of self-care. For a time your feelings may not agree with this reframing, and that's OK. As you continue to practice exercising discretion to limit your exposure to people who mistreat you, your system will gradually adhere to this cognitive reframe. That is to say, your feelings will likely catch up with this mental reframe when you are being reinforced in safe relationships.

If someone is treating you poorly despite your efforts to treat them well, you are entitled to move away from them. After surviving narcissistic abuse as the scapegoat, this is likely an unfamiliar experience, but one well worth practicing.

30

How to Overcome Guilt after Leaving a Narcissistic Abuser

> *Why can it feel harder to create distance from a narcissistic parent than a good-enough parent?*
> *Do you get struck by visions of your narcissistic parent being a sympathetic victim to your "cruel act" of abandoning them?*
> *Is it hard to separate your happiness from that of others?*

The term "narcissistic abuse" is pretty recognizable as a bad thing. No one is going to sign up for any form of abuse, right? So, if you are unfortunate enough to know such abuse firsthand, how can it be that the prospect of leaving your abuser can feel scarier and more conflictual and guilt-inducing than staying in the abusive situation? In this chapter, I will explain how to overcome the guilt you may feel in the process of trying to leave a narcissist.

Where the Guilt Comes From

If you grew up with a narcissistic parent, you likely had to deal with a pretty consistent experience of emotional deprivation despite constantly working hard to give to your parent. At the same time, you may have been accused of not giving anything, being thoughtless, inconsiderate, and so on. Although you felt like you were giving and getting little to nothing in return, the external reality you shared with your narcissistic abuser was woven into their claims that you didn't give enough despite how much they—supposedly—gave to you. It can be confusing.

Making the Narcissist Happy with You

Often in the course of narcissistic abuse, you are pressured to think that the only way to survive is to make the narcissistic abuser happy with you. For the child, this is an easy sell, because they need the parent to give to them the necessary ingredients to feel loved for who they are as separate people in the world and to feel like their own love is valuable to others. The child fears that if their own parent does not offer them this, then they will never find it in their lifetime. The narcissist feels unconsciously entitled to others' efforts to make them happy because they believe that they are more important than others. This is why the experience in the relationship can feel so one-sided, despite the fact that the narcissistic abuser seems so convinced that you're not giving them enough.

One way to make such a relationship with a narcissist parent sort of work is to assume responsibility for their emotional well-being. They child may consciously or unconsciously reason that the narcissist's happiness is more important than their own. They can now regard their own happiness as proof that they are as selfish as the narcissistic parent claims they are. This is an adaptive maneuver to avoid the other outcome of having no way to attach to the very person they so desperately need. It allows them to avoid feeling catastrophically alone.

The Narcissistic Abuser's Happiness Takes the Place of Your Own

The trade-off for this strategy is that now the narcissistic abuser's happiness takes the place of your own. Doing something that promotes your own needs for protection and happiness—such as putting distance between you and the narcissistic abuser—can initially feel like something that would break the narcissistic abuser. It flies in the face of the belief that you are first and foremost responsible for their happiness—before your own. I believe that defying this rule may be one source of guilt. This may be akin to what a sin feels like if you're religious. The survivor has had to elevate the importance of the narcissistic abuser—just like a believer would with their god—and anything that goes against the "commandments" of that elevated deity would feel like a transgression.

There is another— I think deeper—reason why you can feel guilt and a whole host of other bad feelings. The initial dilemma with a narcissistic parent was that you cared more about attaching to them than they were able to care about attaching to you—through no fault of your own. Nonetheless, if you hadn't figured out how to take responsibility for their emotional well-being as a compensatory strategy, you would have been and felt completely abandoned.

I think our systems are designed to prevent such psychological catastrophes from happening, and one way of doing that is to send aversive signals when we move away from this makeshift form of one-sided attachment toward something that is hopefully more fulfilling and reciprocal. So, feelings of guilt, extreme anxiety, or even terror can often arise when you contemplate psychological separation from the narcissistic abuser. These feelings are well-documented in the psychoanalytic literature, and in a lot of ways, this is what therapy is designed to do: offer support, understanding, and a supportive relationship as you traverse the emotional terrain from the "bad old way" of attaching to the "new, untrodden good way" of attaching to others.

How to Overcome Guilt When Leaving Your Narcissistic Abuser

Here are three strategies to challenge the feelings of guilt that can emerge when separating from a narcissistic parent.

Know That Your Guilt Comes from Feeling Responsible for Someone Else

First, you can arm yourself with the understanding that your guilt stems from the assumption of responsibility for the narcissistic abuser's emotional well-being. With this in mind, you can work to compassionately understand why you had to assume this responsibility in the first place. Next, you can gently challenge this premise—what would it mean if you were not responsible for them in this manner? Why are their needs more important than your own? It may feel like that's the case, but what's the objective evidence to suggest they are? As you practice extending your attention to the information generated in such thought exercises, you may begin to feel safer and far less guilty as you proceed to separate from your abuser.

Connect to Safe People and Communities

Second is making sure you have connections to other safe people and communities. This can reduce the deep fear, anxiety, and guilt that comes with moving away from the only way you've known attachment to feel. The goal is to know that, although it feels similar to the trauma of separating from someone who does not treat you well, you're in a different situation today. You have people who are genuinely interested in and care about how you feel as the separate unique person you are. You can find this in the form of friendships, romantic relationships, and/or online communities.

Know You Deserve Your Own Patience and Compassion

Third, this is a process, not a switch that's flipped. As best you can, offer yourself patience, kindness, and compassion as you take incremental steps toward your goal. It is a barge you're trying to turn around—not a sailboat—so doing it safely and successfully requires a persistent, patient, and steady hand.

31

Giving up the Quest to Be Important to the Narcissist

> *Have you had a parent or partner in your life whose approval you wanted so badly, but it always seemed out of reach?*
> *Did life feel more exciting or even more worth living when you were in the company of this person and much less so when away from him or her?*
> *Has the quest to be important to the narcissist felt consuming yet impossible to achieve?*

If you answered yes to any of these questions, you may have experienced narcissistic abuse that preyed upon your hope for authentic connection to others. In this chapter, I will explain how the quest to be important to the narcissist can become all-consuming. Your pursuit of connection and hope to be important to your abuser is used by them to inflate their own self-worth rather than connect to you. They do this by being seeing you as wanting to be with them more than they want to be with you.

Once I have explored this, I will offer an exercise to help you identify if you are in—or have been—in a relationship like this or not.

How the Quest to Be Important to the Narcissist Begins

There are at least two ways that a survivor can become wrapped up in getting a narcissist to see them as important. The first is via admiration. If the narcissistic parent is someone whom you find yourself admiring for seeming to possess a certain quality, then the reflex of looking up to this person can kick in. If this person absorbs your admiration without offering much in return, you may feel like you're not worth being admired by them or—if it continues long enough—by yourself. That feels bad, obviously. It is that conspicuous feeling of worthlessness that is often the telltale sign you are in a relationship with a narcissistic abuser. When the person you admire doesn't offer you anything in return and you grow to feel worthless in relation to them, a vicious cycle can get set up.

Once this dynamic is in place, the only way to relieve yourself of your feelings of worthlessness is to further pursue the narcissist with the hope that they might eventually grant you access to their privileged circle of (seeming) self-worth. It might feel like you can finally like and admire yourself once you are deemed important to the narcissist. As a result, the impetus can be to abandon yourself and what is important to you because that feels bad and instead seeking what feels fleetingly good—applauding the narcissist for their specialness.

How to Surrender the Quest

I think the way out of this torturous yet enticing arrangement with the narcissist is to work your way back to the place that felt imperative to leave: your own experience. The fuel for this cycle is when you start to feel a sense of worthlessness in relation to the narcissist. Next, you determine that worthlessness can only be resolved by becoming important to them. So, the cycle breaks when we return to the place we felt we had to leave. It can be useful to do this with the understanding that you see and experience yourself to be unworthy of your own attention because you've been influenced to think about yourself in this way as a product of being close to a narcissistic abuser.

In other words, don't really think you're not important enough to pay attention to as you are, but you've been treated in ways to deliberately make you think this is true. Nonetheless, the feelings that emerge when you give up the quest to be important to the narcissist can be difficult to endure. You may feel an initial sense of hopelessness, confusion, or even disorientation. The pursuit of being important to the narcissistic person may have served an organizing function for you, so giving it up may feel a little disorganizing at first. But this can be like clearing the decks so that something much sturdier and lasting can develop from within.

As you notice, accept, and begin to champion what's inside you, you will begin to seek relationships that complement this. This is different from seeking relationships that let you forget yourself and the bad feelings that can accompany being aware of yourself.

Are You Caught Trying to Be Important to a Narcissist?

Here are a series of statements about someone you suspect may be playing this role in your life. Ask yourself if they are true. You can respond with "most of the time," "sometimes," or "never."

- I feel more like myself when I am with this person
- This person works to understand me where I am at
- This person values our friendship/relationship and shows me that
- This person values what I offer them as a friend, partner, or child
- This person shows interest in and supports what's important to me—even when they have no personal interest in the matter
- This person knows me
- This person sees me as an intact person
- I am important to this person
- If I need help, I feel good about asking this person for it

If you selected *sometimes* or *never* on any of these items, it may be worth examining this relationship and considering some of what was discussed in this chapter. Ultimately, the goal is to enter and maintain relationships that allow you to feel like yourself and move away from relationships where that is not offered.

32

Giving up the Quest to Prove the Narcissist Wrong About You

> *Does it feel like you can't feel good about yourself until you prove your narcissistic parent's accusations were wrong?*
>
> *Do you carry an inner sense of being defective that needs to be disproven before you can feel deserving of what you want?*
>
> *Do you feel hopeless when you consider that you may never get your narcissistic parent to see you in a good light?*

When you're a kid and you have no choice but to bond with a narcissistic parent, and that parent uses you as a receptacle for their own feelings of worthlessness, you can walk around having to believe some pretty terrible things about yourself. Life can feel like it is rigged against you, as if nothing you do ever warrants a feeling of credit, accomplishment, or pride. Like no matter how hard you work in therapy, engaging in self-exploration and the like, feelings of self-worth and optimism are elusive.

In this chapter, I explain how this experience can be driven by a wish to prove the narcissistic parent wrong about you. This is a powerful reflex when we've been mistreated by someone who is important to us, but I will explain how you get to enjoy even more power within yourself when you exit the debate on your worth with the narcissistic parent. Next, I will offer a daily practice you can incorporate to help yourself give up the struggle to prove the narcissist wrong, and in so doing, realize how right you have been all along.

The Quest to Prove the Narcissist Wrong

If you've had to bond with a narcissistic parent, you may have had to live life as though you were starting a race fifty yards back from the starting line. This is especially likely to be the case when the other parent either is not home or is so psychologically compromised that they do not offer you a viable relationship to trust and invest in. The kind of narcissistic parent I am talking about would likely fit the mold of what is known as a covert narcissist.

This type of narcissistic personality still copes with their intolerable feelings of worthlessness by believing themselves to be more important or special than others. However, they do so under the guise of being agreeable, helpful, and "having it all together." For the child in a family where the narcissistic parent seems stable and the other parent volatile, hypocritical, or obviously unviable to look up to, the narcissist is often the child's only choice when seeking attachment. Of course, the same can happen if there is no other parent, as is the case in single-parent households.

Although the narcissistic parent may seem to be worth the child's admiration, he or she is still incapable of offering them the reciprocity, care, and sense of being important that they need to develop a healthy sense of self. Instead, as a child you may find it necessary to idealize someone who seems to have no need for you, is utterly indifferent to your inner world, and only responds to you when it suits their need to feel better about themselves. And yet all of this, for the kid, is still felt to be infinitely better than having no parent. The experience of having no one—and in essence, being no one to anybody—is one that must be avoided at all costs.

The child of a narcissistic parent in this situation can be left believing they are defective, unimportant, and not worth being listened to. One common way they may cope is to organize their lives in ways designed to disprove these things about themselves. This can look like an unrelenting drive to achieve. The feeling that one's ideas are not worth listening to is a humiliating one, especially when you suspect you have good ideas. The result, then, can be an inner world where you feel generally bad about who you are, but a promise is always held out that if you do a little more, achieve a little more, you will feel important in a lasting way. Although this coping style is absolutely necessary in order to find purpose when the abuse is going on, it leaves the survivor feeling dissatisfied, because the promises never come to fruition. When we have to undertake something to prove our worth to someone who is motivated to see us as worthless, it is impossible to feel fulfilled by it. And yet, when we are treated poorly by someone we have no choice but to believe, it is a very human reaction to want to prove them wrong.

Jarrett came to therapy complaining of feelings of low self-worth and a sense of flatness or meaninglessness in his life. He grew up in a family with a very emotionally volatile mother who would alternately have fits of rage, act sweet toward Jarrett, or grow sullen and despairing. Jarrett said he saw her as someone to watch his step around, but not someone he could ever rely on.

In contrast, Jarrett described his father as someone he had always looked up to. He had been in the military and earned some distinctions as an officer, was always very well put together, and was preoccupied with making their house look "perfect" on nights and weekends. When Jarrett's therapist asked about his relationship with his father, he looked a little puzzled. He'd never really thought about it.

At first, Jarrett said he'd always felt lucky just to be around his father in whatever capacity he would allow. As therapy proceeded, Jarrett felt more connected to the therapist, and that seemed to open up more awareness of how he actually felt about their relationship. In one session, Jarrett's made his boldest statement: "I could be sitting right next to my father, but I always felt like I wasn't there! I felt so insignificant to him." Jarret's father had never shown any curiosity about what Jarrett thought or felt. As a result, Jarrett concluded that he was not worth being listened to.

The only two ways Jarrett could remember his father being lively in his interactions with Jarrett was when he was making fun of or correcting him.

As an eight-year-old, if Jarrett grew tired of the incessant list of chores he was asked to do around their home every weekend and complained, a big smile would spread across his father's face. He would mockingly say, "Oh what is it, Mr. Whiner? I know you don't want to do this, do you? Oh, poor Mr. Whiner."

What Jarrett hated most about these episodes was that he was actually glad that his father was coming forward and making some sort of contact with him. He found himself laughing along with his father at his own expense. Still, it felt so much better than the general feeling of abandonment he otherwise constantly felt in relation to his father.

The other way Jarrett's father seemed to spring into action was when he had a problem that his father could take pleasure in fixing. If all was going well in Jarrett's life, his father would show no interest in him at all. One time Jarrett brought home a report card full of As, with one A-. His father looked at it, tossed it dismissively on the counter, and rhetorically asked, "What's with the minus?" before walking out of the kitchen, uninterested in Jarrett's response. But when Jarrett was struggling with math and could ask his father for help, his father would come alive to him again. Jarrett recalled thwarting his successes at school, presenting himself as being in need of tutoring so that he'd have some way of eking out a feeling of connection with his father.

Jarrett grew to understand that the only form of relationship available to him was with someone he looked up to but who treated him as if he were insignificant, not worth listening to, deserving of mockery, and defective. As a result, he *learned to believe these things about himself. But to Jarrett's credit, he made his life about trying to find a way to disprove these painful conclusions. He worked really hard in school to get good grades and get into a good college even though internally he couldn't feel satisfied or proud of himself for doing so. He also labored to prove to himself that he deserved to be and feel respected by the people in his life. He did this despite always feeling like he was in an uphill battle and that others' default way of viewing him was that he was insignificant and deserving of their mockery. I think it was his will to fight these conclusions that made therapy prove so helpful once he got into it. Now he could see how fallacious these beliefs were, and that they had been a means to the end of trying to get a minimal amount of care from a father who was disinclined to offer any.*

As Jarrett grew to compassionately see why and how he'd had to adopt these beliefs about himself, he felt freed from the tyranny of always having to work to prove them wrong. His life loosened up quite a bit. Toward the end of one session, he said, "You know, I realize that so much of what I did before was to get relief from this terrible feeling I always used to have. Like if I was not being productive or doing something I thought made me important, then I felt totally insignificant and worthless. Now, that feeling does not rule me. I still feel it at times, but I don't have to run from it or do something immediately to make it go away. Now, I can experience and ask myself what I want to do right now . . . not to make the feeling go away but because it is important to me. I guess I have the right version of 'me' in my mind now."

Jarrett's case illustrates how you can work to surrender the mission of proving the narcissistic parent wrong about yourself. Although things might feel hopeless at the outset, there can be a tremendous amount to gain by doing so. The hopelessness you may feel giving up on this mission is not the hopelessness of never feeling pride or self-worth. Rather, I believe it is the accurate hopelessness of never feeling as close and connected to your narcissistic parent as you were born wanting. As that conclusion is accepted, other sources of connection—namely, safe people—grow to seem more valuable and capable of filling the void that was left by the emotional deprivation suffered at the hands of the narcissistic parent.

Pillar #3:

Defy the Narcissist's Rules

33

Measure the Long Road to Recovery

> *Do you wonder how long it takes to recover from being the scapegoat child to a narcissistic parent?*
> *What are the factors that go into determining the answer to this question?*
> *Is it sometimes a struggle to keep your morale up without a sense of how long it will take before living feels better?*

In my experience, this topic comes up a lot with survivors of narcissistic abuse. And how could it not? If you have to live under the auspices of the grim self-diminishing beliefs you had to adapt to survive narcissistic abuse, then of course you want to know how long it will be until you can expect some relief. I often engage with this question as people are considering or beginning therapy to recover from narcissistic abuse. In this chapter, I discuss three factors that can determine the answer.

I want to clarify that these answers are based on my clinical, professional, and personal experience. These answers can be thought of as hypotheses and would benefit from actual research with survivors of narcissistic abuse to see if they are correct. With that being said, I believe three factors determine how long it takes to recover from narcissistic abuse.

How Early Did the Narcissistic Abuse Start?

If you were born to a narcissistic parent, for example, and had the misfortune of having to forge your beliefs about who you are and what you can expect from others with someone so self-absorbed, then more time will be needed to recover. In contrast, if you had a good-enough relationship with at least one caregiver where you felt protected, cared for, interesting, and loved, and the narcissistic abuse occurred later in your life, recovery may not take as long.

Here's why. In the early stages of life, we are dependent on our primary caregivers to meet our physical, psychological, and emotional needs. These include being adequately fed, diapered, comforted, played with, and cared for. A young child is self-centered and, in a healthy family, expects their parents to complement their self-centeredness with support, admiration, appreciation, and love. The family delights in the child's discovery of themselves and their world. Such a child will develop beliefs that others are available, generous, and appreciative of who they are in a fairly unconditional way, and that they are deserving of care, protection, and love.

Let's say someone with this type of childhood is now in their twenties and finds a romantic partner who initially is devoted, charismatic, admiring, admirable, and seemingly all that the person hoped for. As time passes, the partner seems to grow bored and subtly starts expressing disdain toward our subject. This derision only increases, and our subject initially works very hard to restore the relationship to its initial bliss and suffers flagging self-worth from feeling unable to do so. After reconnecting with some longtime friends and family members, our subject realizes that it is not he but the partner who is the problem. Our subject sees that his partner is treating him in ways that are at odds with his beliefs about who he is, how he should be treated, and what he deserves. This person might break up with their narcissistic partner in short order and recover from the effects of the abuse relatively quickly.

In this example, our subject had had the fortune of forging self-worth and enhancing fundamental beliefs about themselves and others in the early parts of his life. When his partner started to reveal their narcissistic ways, they *conflicted with* our subject's beliefs about himself. That conflict allowed him to identify what was happening after reconnecting with friends and family and to know he deserved better.

In contrast, someone who forged their beliefs about themselves and others with a narcissistic parent at the beginning of life had the misfortune of learning that their needs were less important than the parent's, that they were undeserving of the care and attention they so badly wanted, and that there was something wrong with them that made them unlovable. If, in their twenties, this person fell into the kind of narcissistic relationship described above, the experience would be quite different. The initial way the narcissistic partner fawned over our subject would have felt strange, and the ensuing criticism and devaluation more familiar. This child of a narcissistic parent would not experience a conflict when being mistreated by the narcissistic partner the way the person with good-enough parents did.

In such cases, a longer time may be required to recover from narcissistic abuse. The beliefs the child of a narcissistic parent developed early in life must be identified and challenged so that current mistreatment grows to feel like something unwarranted rather than expected. I would say that long-term therapy is an important option to consider if you find yourself in this boat. Participation in new, safe relationships is the most critical ingredient to recovery from narcissistic abuse. Good, ongoing therapy can help the survivor reprogram the beliefs held to date and work out new beliefs that enhance, rather than diminish, your quality of life.

Did Anyone Protect You from the Narcissistic Abuse?

Suppose you were born into a family with a narcissistic parent whose authority went unquestioned. In that case, you may have had to adopt beliefs about your unworthiness and the narcissistic parent's superiority in a more intense way. As a result, recovery can take longer.

Often a narcissistic parent will choose a spouse who enables their need to be admired, in control at all times, and entitled. This spouse may be prone to idealizing others and possess low self-worth. I am talking about the family role of the enabler parent discussed in Chapter 7.

If you had a narcissistic parent and the other parent was an enabler, you missed out on having another adult to appeal to for protection and to model healthy disagreement with the narcissistic parent's demands. Instead, you may have had to conclude that the narcissistic parent should be taken seriously no matter how self-absorbed and abusive they acted toward you. The family's job in such tragic circumstances is to prevent the narcissistic parent's behavior from being exposed to the wider community. To seek protection from outside the family can feel like leaving the only reality the child knows, and may be nearly impossible.

Suppose you benefitted from having another adult who saw your narcissistic parent for who they were and offered you a reliable connection. In such cases, you got to experience a frame of reference that felt legitimate yet did not require you to compromise in the way the narcissistic parent required. You may have even expressed your disillusionment at this parent to this other adult or heard them express theirs. All of this can be extremely useful to the eventual process of recovery and may reduce the time it takes for you to recover from the narcissistic abuse.

How Long Did the Narcissistic Abuse Last?

The duration of the narcissistic abuse you survived can impact how much your system had to accommodate this mistreatment. A child who had to be vigilant of and prepared for his narcissistic father's outbursts of rage at the slightest show of "disrespect" may understandably have a nervous system wired for ongoing threats. On a fundamental level, living can feel like being under siege when this has been your reality from the start of life and adolescence.

In contrast, someone who had a safe enough environment as a young child will have the benefit of experiencing a time when being narcissistically abused was not their reality. Their nervous systems may have different ways of regulating instead of expecting constant threats.

34

Reclaim What You Sacrificed

> *Do you feel estranged from the positive ways in which other people seem to experience you?*
> *Does it seem like every measure of success you achieve is pure luck?*
> *Do you tell yourself that people who like you don't know the "real you"?*

Most scapegoat survivors of narcissistic abuse struggle to know they can safely experience themselves as they actually are. They've had to don a costume of being abhorrent to the people who they first met in life and tragically learned how dangerous it was to take off that costume. The crux of recovery from being the scapegoat in a family structured around a parent's narcissism is experiencing a sense of safety in existing as you actually are, without the costume. To recover from narcissistic abuse, it is vital to reclaim what you had to sacrifice.

What do I mean by a costume? There is a coercive, orchestrated—even theatrical—element to the role of being a scapegoat child to the narcissistic parent. Most scapegoat children have told themselves at one point or another, "My parent wouldn't hurt me like this if I were not so bad." In order to enter into this role, the child has to wear the costume of the scapegoat. The child may even have to forget that it is a costume and confuse the garment for their own skin.

At some point in life, it becomes possible to notice that you have worn and are wearing the scapegoat costume. Then, you get to see how much the costume masks—that there is so much to who you are that is totally at odds with the scapegoat role. In fact, these features of you may have always seemed out of reach to you while in the costume. You may look at others who seem to be strong, dignified, and worthy of respect and love only to see that you yourself have had those traits all along. It is not that you had to figure out how to obtain these wanted traits; instead, you realize that your suffering has come from having to tell yourself you do not have what you in fact possess. The costume would not allow it. You couldn't know that you were attractive because the costume said you were hideous. You couldn't know your own courage because the costume said you were a coward. You couldn't know your own dignity because the costume said you were of lower status.

In this chapter, I describe the process of reclaiming what you have had to sacrifice within yourself to play the role of scapegoat. This reclamation project is often met with deeply felt pangs of fear. I offer some explanations of where the danger that leads to the fear comes from. Next, I provide strategies for coping with this fear. Last, I describe a major shift in your purpose for living that occurs when you have reclaimed your sense of safety in being your positive and strong self.

Recovery from narcissistic abuse can be confusing. It is important to keep in mind that, for the scapegoat survivor, what can feel most dangerous is considering positive things about themselves. If you've had the misfortune of being scapegoated by a narcissistic parent, there are very real survival mechanisms in place that prevent you from believing your own mother or father could have been unfair in how they treated you. The child's psychological survival requires that they believe they have a parent who is willing to care for them. If that parent is frightening or hurtful—and there are no other viable adults to attach to—it creates a problem, and the child has no one to help them solve it. The child's solution is often to wear the costume of scapegoat as the narcissistic parent requires while forcing themselves to believe that the parent knows what is best.

Given such early circumstances, it stands to reason that becoming aware of your strengths as a person might feel dangerous. Crediting yourself with admirable traits would be at odds with the costume that you used to ensure a very important form of survival. And yet here you are, looking for a way to cure your inner sense of pain, muzzled agony, emptiness, and confusion. One way to orient yourself is to, when you experience heightened bad feelings, ask yourself if you have done or thought something that gave credit to who you are as a person. If you are a scapegoat survivor, bad feelings may get triggered by such positive thoughts about yourself. That sequence was exactly what let you survive earlier.

If you find that you tend to feel particularly bad after feeling good about yourself, that's great, because now you have identified very fertile ground to work on in your recovery. With this awareness, you can work to notice the thoughts that might intervene between the good feelings and the bad feelings.

> Bruce was a writer who was in therapy after surviving a childhood where he was the scapegoat to a narcissistic mother. She had to see him as incapable and in need of her help at all costs. Bruce learned that if he started to build momentum in something he was doing, he had to appear feckless and confused, or she would have felt outdone by him. When that happened, she would viciously berate, undermine, and attack him for some made-up reason.
>
> In therapy one day, Bruce reported that he'd completed an entire chapter on the novel he was working on. In the next session, he came in deflated and said he'd completely lost his mojo in the past week. His mind was scattered, and he kept feeling distracted. His therapist inferred that his use and acknowledgement of his actual prowess as a writer may have set off this bout of self-disparagement. His therapist said, "I wonder if something didn't feel quite right—or maybe safe—after you told me how well the writing was going last week?"
>
> Bruce said, "What do you mean? Why wouldn't that feel safe? I was feeling good."
>
> Therapist: "I know you were. But I also know that, in the past, you figured out some pretty painful ways to contort yourself so that you were seen as incapable or directionless and in need of being told what to do. That's a lot like the state you seem to find yourself in now."

Bruce: "Yeah, you're right. But I don't know what to do about this."

Therapist: "Well, acknowledging that it might be happening is a really important first step. Seeing how things are operating now suggests that they could be different in the future. As you think back on leaving session last week, can you pay attention to any thoughts you may have had about telling me about your success with the chapter?"

Bruce: "Well . . . I remember feeling some sort of dis-ease. It is hard to put into words, but something didn't quite feel right. Then I went home and tried to write more and was at a complete loss."

Therapist: "Yes, that dis-ease seems to have been a warning signal from your past that you were in dangerous territory. By demonstrating your competence, you were doing something that this part of you associates with losing someone you really needed at the time and maybe incurring their wrath."

Bruce: "Yeah, I see that. But what can I do about it?"

Therapist: "You can perhaps try to mimic what we are doing now: paying attention to this part of you that's concerned about what will happen if you know your strengths, offering that part of you your compassionate understanding, then providing the new information that you are now safe. You're in the clear. You get to write to your full potential without the reprisal you used to have to steel yourself for."

Now, Bruce's struggles with his writing did not disappear in one fell swoop. But he began to pay attention to the pangs of fear that arose when he brandished aspects of who he was in life. Next, he offered himself validation and compassion. He would remind himself that he was no longer dependent on his mother, nor vulnerable to her attacks. Over time, and with a lot of patience with himself, he got to experience longer and longer periods of sustained writing. This translated to longer periods of connecting with himself while feeling safe in doing so. Over the course of a few years, Bruce's main purpose shifted from avoiding the post-traumatic danger of being caught without the scapegoat costume to experiencing the rewards of exercising his strengths as a person.

This example highlights another key ingredient in knowing it is safe to reclaim what you once had to sacrifice to recover from narcissistic abuse: the presence of a new relationship where the scapegoat costume is not necessary. Bruce knew his therapist had his best interests at heart, and therefore wouldn't want him to wear the costume. Such relationships can also happen outside the therapy office.

As illustrated with Bruce, when you have experienced enough safety in being your real and positive self, a shift may occur. What the scapegoat survivor was initially denied by his or her narcissistic parents becomes achievable—the prospect of living to experience the firsthand meaning and gratification of being who you were meant to be in this world. You undertake endeavors because they feel aligned with who you know yourself to be rather than solely as a means to the end of avoiding a post-traumatic danger. I am talking about this not to discount the value of the effort it takes to get to a point where such self-congruence is not yet safe to experience. Rather, I am hoping that fleshing out what life after reclaiming yourself looks like can serve a hopeful function.

35

Fight for Your Right to Have Fun

> *Do you find yourself finding excuses not to do things that you know you enjoy?*
> *Does anything that isn't work or school feel like something you should not be doing?*
> *Is it strange to see other people having fun? Like how is it that they are so happy?*

When I was in fourth grade, this incredible Beastie Boys album, *Licensed to Ill*, came out. One of the best tracks on it was called "Fight for Your Right to Party." If you haven't heard it, give it a listen—it's awesome. What struck me was how brazenly the Beasties were championing their right to have fun in the song. I grew up in a home that was a lot like the ones I talk about in this book, so the notion of putting your right to have fun squarely in the center of your life and doing everything in your power to protect it was pretty foreign to me—but super appealing. If you have suffered narcissistic abuse from a parent or a partner, it is no accident that having fun, and prioritizing it in your life, can feel like a foreign and even dangerous concept.

I want to discuss why fun is an endangered species for the survivor of narcissistic abuse, and how you can work to know you deserve it and that it is safe to experience in your recovery process.

Why It Can Be Dangerous to Have Fun Around Your Narcissistic Abuser

The narcissist needs to see the scapegoat victim of their relocated worthlessness living a grim, colorless life. This reinforces their conviction that the scapegoat does not deserve anything better than the treatment they are getting, which allows the narcissist to function with a more intact—if brittle—sense of themselves.

What happens if the scapegoat dares to experience fun, and shows a sign of life and color in their demeanor? This can completely upend the narcissist's fragile control over their artificially inflated sense of self-worth. To see a scapegoat victim smiling and enjoying themselves in response to something that is unrelated to the narcissist can send the message that they think they deserve better in their lives and that their happiness is worth something. All these messages can feel profoundly threatening to the narcissist.

How will they cope? Well, when you are a hammer, everything looks like a nail, and the narcissist is a psychological one-trick pony when it comes to handling threats to their self-esteem—they seek to devalue or even destroy the threat. Survivors of such abuse can often recall particularly wrathful attacks during times when it was evident they were having fun in their lives. Being picked up from a party while laughing with friends could mean getting yelled at for not doing chores once those friends had been dropped off. Going to a school dance and coming home a minute late could create an avalanche of accusations and punishment. And so on.

> *One scapegoat survivor recalled how, in sixth grade, his social world began to open up, and his narcissistic mother grew intent on preventing him from enjoying it. She would make up chores just as he was about to leave to meet his friends and forbid him from joining them. As he thought of the years ahead of him, he fretted over how he could possibly obtain the freedoms that other teenagers seemed to have without getting into World War III at home.*
>
> *That year, two older students came to talk to his class about what to expect in high school. He raised his hand and asked how they had been able to convince their parents to allow them to drive in cars with friends or go to parties. The high school students kind of shrugged, and he realized this was not a struggle for them in their homes.*

For fear of the narcissist's reaction, the scapegoat has to learn to wean themselves off of fun. It is just too dangerous. One way to do this is to grow to see fun as immoral or bad, and only accomplishment as worthy of one's effort. Of course, this attitude may serve the primary function of appearing grim in view of the narcissistic parent or partner. Similar to Cinderella, where every moment has to be filled up with tedious housework of some sort. You may recall how Cinderella's mother and stepsisters took particular delight in seeing her furiously scrubbing floors and sweeping, growing aghast and contemptuous when her foot fit the glass slipper.

How to Feel Safe to Have Fun Again

During recovery, it is essential to have enough protective distance between you and your narcissistic abuser so that experimenting with different strategies does not make you vulnerable to further attack. Assuming this distance is in place, you might notice you are habitually avoiding the experience of fun.

You may feel anxious or ill-at-ease within when in an unstructured setting with friends, or be planning your time so that you're always in the process of going after a goal. It can be useful to prescribe yourself activities designed for no other purpose than to have fun, like watching a sunset, taking a directionless long walk, or having an extended lunch with a friend. The idea is not to find these activities fun right away, but with their continued inclusion in your day-to-day experience, you might get reacquainted with the experience of fun.

I want to make one important note about fighting for your right to party in the process of recovery from narcissistic abuse. Fun is innocent and connects us to our basic humanity. Engaging in activities just because they bring you a measure of joy can bring into stark contrast how your humanity has been denigrated by the narcissistic abuser. It can bring home that, at your core, you are very good and decent being, and that the lies you had to believe to survive the narcissistic abuse were never true. This can evoke a lot of grief. I don't think there's anything that can or should be done about such grief. As a very dear friend of mine used to say, this is "clean" pain, as opposed the dirty pain that can come with avoiding such grief.

36

Reclaim Your Voice

> *Do you have difficulty knowing what you want for yourself?*
>
> *Do relationships seem to be all about what the other person wants and needs?*
>
> *Do you have to curate what you say before you say it for fear of not being understood?*

If you answered yes to any of these questions and you identify as the scapegoat to a narcissistic parent, you may have had to muzzle your own voice to survive. In this chapter, I describe how and why this muzzle can be necessary for a child tasked with attaching to a narcissistic parent. Next, I describe how this muzzle can show up in adulthood. Third, I address the role of shame in keeping the muzzle affixed to yourself.

> *Stacey came to therapy due to pervasive anxiety. No matter what she did in her life, she always felt an underlying sense of dis-ease, self-criticism, and self-doubt. It didn't seem to matter whether others liked her or what she was doing. Her private experience felt unendingly stormy.*

She felt particularly ill at ease in interaction with others. When she would come into contact with someone else, she would immediately feel exquisitely aware of what they might be thinking, feeling, and most importantly, needing. She could only be someone who provided for that person's needs. She would smile to convey that she valued their presence. She would display intense interest in what they were saying. She would allow whatever the other person was describing to intrude on her own thoughts.

Of course, none of these experiences were in and of themselves problematic—it was the "or else" quality that Stacey felt when they came about. Internally, she felt mandated to respond and dote on other people, or something calamitous would happen. It was as if her deep biological programming told her to do this, and she was just along for the ride. In therapy, she eventually became able to express her long-held resentment at having to lose herself in this way when she came into contact with others. She had difficulty staying seated in herself long enough to know what she preferred, wanted, or needed in these interactions. Like during an eclipse, the other became the moon that blocked the light of her inner self's sun.

During sessions, Stacey used her therapist's continued focus on her and seeming ability to take care of his own emotional needs to offer herself a compassionate understanding of why she had found it so necessary to muzzle her own voice. This supportive experience that allowed her to take up space let her see how her mother had demanded her complete focus growing up.

Stacey's mother had been particularly volatile and prone to rage if she did not feel superior, admired, and all-powerful at all times. Since such states of supremacy are hard to consistently come by for human beings, Stacey had to endure her mother's rage attacks on a near daily basis. She kept hope alive by telling herself that, if she could predict and take care of her mother's moods and needs, she could prevent the next rage attack. In therapy, she was able to offer herself comfort, as she no longer feared being attacked if she did not engage in prioritizing her therapist's needs and muzzling her own.

Are Relationships All about the Other Person's Needs?

Stacey's is a story of muzzling, then freeing, her voice. The dangerous conditions with her mother made it necessary to muzzle her voice in the first place, but once she was under emotionally safe conditions with her therapist, she was able to begin to recover her it. For Stacey and others with a narcissistic parent, the demands from the parent are all about the parent. The child's own needs constitute a wild card that the parent does not consider or genuinely care about. Instead, if the child's inserts their needs into the relationship with the narcissistic parent, they may be met with rebuke, attack, humiliation, and worse. It can become necessary for the child to put a figurative muzzle over their authentic voice for two reasons: it spares the child from some of these attacks and may evoke a measure of goodwill from the narcissistic parent.

By voice, I mean one's own unique and original actions, opinions, preferences, and needs in the world. You can think of an infant who is with their good-enough parent. That infant might have all kinds of movements emanating from within: looking all around them, grabbing at objects or people of interest, and so on. If the child learns that what comes from within is usually met in a benign way, they procedurally learn that it is safe to listen to and act from the signals within themselves. If others react to the child as if his actions deserve rejection, the child will learn to distrust his inner signals, drown them out, and pay more attention to and prioritize the signals coming from others.

The Role of Shame in Muzzling the Scapegoat Survivor's Voice

Shame is often employed to keep one's inner voice from intruding into the relationship with the narcissistic parent. This emotion results when we are expecting to be met with welcome, understanding, and appreciation and are instead regarded as distasteful objects. The person on the receiving end of this unanticipated bad reception can feel intense aggression toward themselves. They may even wish they could get away from their very existence. That's also what happens to the child whose narcissistic parent regards the child's voice, needs, and actions as taking away from the parent's own artificial sense of dominance and superiority. Now the child who is hoping and expecting to be met with excitement is instead met with scorn and contempt for showing who they really are. They experience a toxic intensity of shame. In order to avoid such emotional trauma, the child can learn to focus more on what others think than what they themselves think.

Here's an example: A seven-year-old child comes home from school with a drawing that she's really proud of. It happens to be raining that day, and she has a little bit of dirt on her boots. As starts to enter the house, she exclaims to her mother, "Mommy, Mommy, look what I drew today!" Her mother does not make eye contact, but says, "Stop. You're going to get mud all over the house! You're always so messy, and you don't think about how that's going to affect other people. Then she walks away.

The little girl is left feeling like she doesn't want to be who she is after being treated this way. If such interactions abound in her relationship with her mother, she will stop paying attention to what makes her happy and excited and wanting to share it with others. Instead, she will see herself through her mother's eyes so that her mother won't find her to be objectionable. She will learn to treat herself like an object, just as the mother does. In doing this, the daughter will have to sacrifice her inner connection to herself. She will grow wary of her spontaneity. The next time she approaches the door after school, she may check herself internally to make sure she is not "too excited." She will begin to exercise more and more caution in expressing what is inside her because her mother's reaction is so painful to her.

How to Remove the Muzzle

The scapegoat child learned to muzzle themselves in a relationship with someone who was not safe to be close to. The way to heal is to have repeated experiences taking the muzzle off in relationships with people who *are* safe to be close to. It is essential to find people who are oriented toward you in a way that is fundamentally different from your narcissistic parent. These people should show appreciation for you just as you are. As you get to experience feeling valued by others for being yourself, the prospect of expressing your voice can feel much safer. You may not even have to convince yourself to do so. Once you feel safe enough in these new relationships, you may organically want to show more of who you are to these people. You may be surprised to find that your openness evokes their respect for you and signals to them that they can share more of themselves with you. Things may feel reciprocal because safe people are way more comfortable in their own skin than narcissists.

Another good way to practice this is in communities of people who have also survived narcissistic abuse as a scapegoat. Such communities can offer you the experience of feeling easily understood and validated in what was unsafe about speaking up in the past. Implicitly you also get the experience of being heard and respected when you speak up in such forums. An example of such a community is the private Facebook group that accompanies my online course on recovery from narcissistic abuse.[6]

---

[6] You can find the course here: https://lp.jreidtherapy.com/narcissistic-abuse-course

37

Recover Your Confidence

> *Do you find yourself full of doubt when you try to make a decision?*
>
> *Do you sometimes feel like an impostor in your own life?*
>
> *Do you question whether you matter?*

If you answered yes to any of these questions, you may have had to sacrifice your own self-confidence to survive narcissistic abuse. Self-confidence cannot be recovered in one fell swoop, but you can create conditions in your life that allow for its gradual emergence. In this chapter, I am going to explain three such conditions.

By practicing these conditions in your life, you might be able to:

- Know that you can make and sustain new safe relationships
- Pursue goals that are important to you
- Believe in yourself even when others disagree with you

The Danger of Self-Confidence for the Scapegoat Child

A good-enough parent is not threatened by their child's abilities and successes. As a result, their children will likely develop a reasonable amount of self-confidence. The playing field is not level for children of narcissists, however. The scapegoat child must be careful not to outdo their narcissistic parent—otherwise, they risk stepping out of the less-than status their narcissistic parent requires. The result is that the scapegoat child can grow up feeling very bad about who they are. In recovery, it becomes possible to learn that these feelings were never theirs.

Upon reflection, survivors can see they were breathing the only air the narcissistic parent allowed them. They had to have some sort of relationship with the parent, but their parent required them to believe they were the problem. It is difficult to feel confident about yourself under those circumstances. This is particularly the case if no other adult intervenes on the child's behalf.

As a survivor recovering from a childhood of having to be less-than, you know somewhere within you that this is all wrong. Otherwise, you probably wouldn't be reading this book. You may be working toward feeling confident in who you are and what you can contribute. Regaining such confidence is integral to knowing that one is equal to others.

Obstacles to Self-Confidence for Survivors of Narcissistic Abuse

The main obstacles are the beliefs about oneself that are incompatible with self-confidence. For example, one survivor believed that if they showed their abilities, others would find out they were a fraud. To avoid such danger, they avoided expressing their talents. Such avoidance interferes with generating experience that can build confidence.

This type of belief may have been 100 percent accurate when living with a narcissistic abuser. Your parent may have reacted to such displays of ability by saying you were "lucky" or "putting on an act." They wanted you to think that you didn't deserve to be confident in yourself.

You might think of your natural self-confidence as a hot spring. A hot spring develops when water heats up below the earth's surface as a result of deep geothermal activity. As it gets hotter, it rises through the cracks between the rocks. Upon reaching the surface, the water comes spurting out of the earth. The scapegoat's self-confidence-thwarting beliefs are like big slabs of rock laid across the rising hot water, there to prevent the confidence from seeing the light of day. However, just like water, it still rises upward. It may just take a bit longer to get there with these beliefs in the way.

Conditions That Can Help You Feel Safer Being Self-Confident Today

Scapegoat survivors learned to suppress their self-confidence, but conditions can be put in place that allow for new learning. You can understand how that suppression was useful at one time, then seek relationships where you feel safe to do otherwise. You can commit to activities you want to do—whether you feel confident or not.

Build Relationships with People Who Are Not Narcissistic

It is important to build relationships with people who are not narcissistic. If your template for relationships is centered around accommodating a narcissist, this may be easier said than done. That is OK. It may take some trial and error to determine who is a safe person and who is not. The goal remains to find and build relationships that do not require you to suppress your self-confidence for things to work.

Put Distance Between Yourself and the Narcissistic Abuser

Get out of harm's way. When we are in close contact with a narcissistic parent, our survival-based mechanisms can kick in. The familiar practice of forbidding yourself to feel confident may arise. Putting distance between yourself and the source of abuse can allow your mind and body to gradually learn you are no longer in danger. By distance, I mean emotional and psychological distance, which may or may not include physical distance.

Experiment with Ways of Living with Confidence

Experiment with living in ways you would if you felt confident. By practicing such activities, you are inviting self-confidence into your experience. The message you are sending yourself is that it is no longer dangerous to feel self-confident. Prescribing yourself daily acts designed to take care of your well-being is a great place to start.

Commit to the Confident Acts

None of these conditions promise to make you feel confident. They either remove an obstacle to feeling confident or get you in the habit of doing things for yourself where confidence might result. There is a good reason for this.

There is a form of therapy called Acceptance and Commitment Therapy (ACT). One of the principles of ACT is that emotions, thoughts, and feelings are inner private events that we have very little control over. We do have control over external events. No matter what is happening on the inside we can still make a ball roll across the floor by kicking it with our foot. We can get into psychological trouble when we try to apply these principles of cause-and-effect that work in the external world to our internal world.

The trouble is that our inner private events do not take kindly to control. If we feel hopeless and try to convince ourselves to feel hopeful this may not work. Then we might feel even more hopeless and so on. The problem – from the point of view of ACT – is not the hopelessness but our attempt to control and essentially avoid the hopelessness. ACT attempts to shift one's focus to where they can exert control – the external world and the actions one takes in it – while accepting where they cannot exert control – in their inner world. It may seem a bit despairing to consider this, but it can eventually be liberating. We get to point ourselves in whatever direction we want in life. The only catch is that we must be willing to experience whatever private events come up as we proceed in that direction.

These three conditions very much fall into this ACT philosophy. You might attempt to apply these tactics in your life while accepting the myriad of feelings and inner states you might experience along with way. That is easier said than done but the good news is that each moment presents a renewed opportunity to do this. As with all of these tactics if this proves too challenging at certain moments, I would strongly advise exercising patience and compassion towards yourself.

38

Go from Human *Doing* to Human *Being*

> *Do you find your moment-to-moment experience depends on what thought you are thinking right now?*
> *Do you carry around a feeling of inner pain, malaise, or general suffering?*
> *Do you find yourself having to operate more like a human doing than a human being?*

In this chapter, I discuss the difference between being versus doing for the scapegoat survivor of narcissistic abuse. Human doing mode is a "thought-of" way of living that can result from enduring narcissistic abuse. It stands in contrast to the mode of being. Living in a mode of being is hard to do. We *can* realize when we are in the human doing mode and bring our attention back to this moment. Again and again. I discuss the specific challenges faced by scapegoat survivors who are seeking to just be. Last, I offer tactics to get reacquainted with each moment as it is rather than how you *think* it is.

This topic is quite subtle, but hopefully it will resonate with your inner experience. There is always much more happening right now in this moment that what we can think or say about it. People have noticed this for ages: Buddhists, philosophers such as Jean-Paul Sartre, and more recently, Eckart Tolle. They explain that human suffering comes about when what we think about our experience takes precedence over what our experience actually is. Sartre calls this "bad faith"; Eckhart Tolle would say we are moving away from our present being. In short, if we are *being*, then thought is a portion of our experience—but not the entirety of it. When we are trapped in thought, our experience of being can feel scary. Being in thinking or doing mode begets more thinking and more doing. When we are in this mode, we often don't want it to stop. Moving away from our thoughts to our immediate experience of ourselves can feel like leaving a safe harbor.

Why the Scapegoat Survivor of Narcissistic Abuse Is Pressured to Think More than to Be

In order to be, a person has to be oriented toward discovering what is in their immediate experience in each unfolding moment. To do this, it has to be safe to discover what is there. A child who has a good-enough parent can take a wait-and-see approach to his inner life. He does not have to tell himself via thought what is happening, what has happened, and what is going to happen. He can notice what he's experiencing and spontaneously express himself. He can trust that his parent will generally be available, curious, and intact if and when he needs them.

Now contrast this with the scapegoat child being blamed for his narcissistic parent's frustrations. Let's say this child falls down and scrapes her knee. Her narcissistic mother had intended to go meet a friend and is angry at the child's need for care in this moment. Instead of comforting her in her pain, the narcissistic mother may yell at her daughter, "Why aren't you ever careful? You never look where you're going, and now look what you did to yourself!"

If the child listened to how she felt in the face of her mother's contempt, she would experience too much hurt to go on. Then, there would be nobody to comfort her. The child may instead cope by moving away from her experience in that present moment and into her thought-based experience. Maybe she will forcefully tell herself, "You're so bad! Mommy loves you and you just have to mess everything up for her." She then has to keep telling herself things along these lines. As soon as she stops thinking them, that other agonizing experience creeps in again. So, she has to think and think and think thoughts of how she is bad and learn to identify with these thoughts. Eventually, her identity can be a thought-of identity. This child does not have a safe enough relationship with her parent to exist in a wait-and-see mode.

What Happens when Scapegoated Children Have to Move toward Their Thought-Of Identity

The thought-of identity is fragile by nature. It exists through thinking, so if we're not thinking, it can feel like we don't exist. The rabbit hole can grow deeper when we feel as though we only exist when thinking certain thoughts, leading it to feel like our inner life is a continual effort to produce. This thought-of identity is artificial yet necessary to identify with during narcissistic abuse.

A thought-of identity can require a continual output of thought to seem real and ongoing. Gaps in thinking are a part of life, but these can become threatening because they mean gaps in being who we think we. The more identified we are with our thought-of identity, the more such gaps must be avoided. The logic is: "I do not want to float off into oblivion (lose my identity), so I am going to cling to this life preserver (thought-of identity). It has spikes on it that hurt all the time, yet I still fear letting go and sinking into oblivion."

Recovery involves taking the risk of letting go of the life preserver and discovering that one is standing on solid ground now. Each person has to make this discovery for him or herself. It cannot be done in thought. It is based in experience.

Why the Scapegoat Has Had to Overidentify with Their Thought-Of Identity

The narcissist has to find the scapegoat child to be worthless and pressures the them to think and act as such. This is a fiction. The scapegoat must go away from their being and toward their thoughts to maintain it. The child knows they are not as bad as the narcissist insists, but cannot know themselves any other way if they are going to stay in relationship to the parent. This requires a lot of investment in their thought-of identity over their present moment experience. As time goes on, the scapegoat can feel so identified with this identity that they fear losing it means losing their existence.

In the case of narcissistic abuse by a parent, a very terrible sequence can get imposed: The child is not seen or loved for his or her being in the world, only seen or recognized when she or he is merged with his or her mind—just like the narcissistic parent is.

For example, a narcissistic father who is merged with his thought-based experience may be trying to actualize the thought-of identity that he is supremely important to himself and others. The child must then merge with thoughts he has that echo his parent's thoughts. For example, he may think, *Oh wow, look how important Dad is. I could never measure up to him. He's the best.* The child has to move away from any of his present experience that diverges from this thought-state—his own experiences of power and effectiveness included.

When this happens often enough, the child's only option for an identity is such thought-based activity. Another drawback to this state is that it can feel very fragile to go out in the world. Life moves too fast to be fully captured in any of our streams of thought. Gaps in thinking are inevitable when interacting with the wider world and can be very painful for the scapegoat child.

Such pain can make the child seek reunion with the narcissistic parent, as that relationship reinforces the child's thought-based identity. This staves off the gaps in the identity that feel so painful, but the child still has to endure the parent's mistreatment. He faces no good choice in this situation.

> *John was in his mid-twenties when he came to therapy to recover from growing up in a family helmed by a narcissistic mother. He recalled how in first grade, he'd taken particular pride in learning to write cursive. He focused and concentrated fully on the task of writing new letters and words. On Fridays, he and his classmates would take a cursive writing test. He always tried his best.*

At the same time, John was being pressured to think of himself in line with the way his narcissistically abusive mother was treating him. She would constantly find fault in what he did or did not do around the house. He began to think of himself as someone who couldn't do anything right. In therapy, we determined that this became his thought-of identity at the time. From there, the only moments he could imagine himself feeling content were in the future. He could think ahead in time and convince himself he would be happy then. He rarely felt happy in the present moment, however.

John offered a story that demonstrated this strategy of looking ahead to something better. When he was in second grade, his grandparents had been visiting from out of town, and his family was celebrating Christmas that Friday after school. He knew that he would be getting a Transformer toy called Shockwave. As he was doing his cursive homework, he felt his mind transport him to what it was going to be like opening his present. He imagined himself playing with Shockwave. These thoughts made his present moment pale in comparison. He stopped trying his best on the cursive test in that moment. Instead he scribbled the rest of it and sat back in his chair to further imagine playing with the toy. He knew that something very sacred within him was getting compromised. He also felt something equally strong pushing him to do this.

As the scapegoat to his narcissistic mother, John had had to abandon his present moment experience during the cursive test. His being mode seemed to indicate that he wanted to do things right, but this was at odds with his mother's attitude that he could do nothing right. In this moment, he had to surrender to her pressures by scribbling the test in exchange for the thoughts about the toy. To have continued writing his cursive test in earnestness would have resulted in losing his thought-of identity as someone who did nothing right. That felt scarier to him than the hit to his self-worth in not being able to get the answers right.

How to Unidentify with the Thought-Of Identity and Increase Connection to Your Being

If you were scapegoated by a narcissistic parent, the second pillar of distance is extremely important. You need such distance to be able to trust that your old thought-based tactics are not still required to survive today.

It is important to approach these processes with patience and compassion toward yourself. They were often necessary to survive the abuse by the narcissist.

With that attitude in place, the process is to notice when our thoughts are going to the past or future and being aware of this. Eckhart Tolle explains that in noticing these thoughts, they get transformed from facts that we are operating from, instead becoming phenomena that we are noticing and thereby have some distance from.

In concrete terms, a meditation practice is a good way to put this into action. Sitting with yourself for ten or more minutes a day can orient you to the being mode.

39

Learn How to Trust

> *Is it hard to believe that others could genuinely care about your feelings?*
>
> *Do you find yourself assuming some sort of ulterior motive when people seem to be committing an act of kindness toward you?*
>
> *Does it feel like care and affection is something that is earned rather than received?*

Scapegoat survivors were betrayed by the people they were supposed to be able to trust the most. They were forced to care more about their narcissistic parent's needs than their own. This may have set them up to be very wary of trusting others. Survivors who had no other adult to bond to may find it particularly difficult. In this chapter, I explain how the scapegoat child was right to be skeptical of the narcissistic parent's displays of affection or approval. Next, I offer three tools to help retire your skepticism when safe people show you sincere care today.

A Narcissistic Parent Leaves the Child Emotionally Malnourished

A narcissistic parent does not possess the empathy nor ability to think and care about your needs. No matter how self-absorbed and punitive the parent was, there would likely have been some good moments now and again—when your parent smiled fondly at you, or showed affection, or spoke highly of you to others. Part of the appeal of such moments may just be that they were not being mean to you. However, you likely sensed that when the narcissist was showing you kindness, there must have been something in it for him or her.

Such affection is not freely given in narcissistic abuse and often comes with a strategic aim. It may be to offset an earlier act of aggression toward you, or set you up to demonstrate how you "take advantage" of the narcissist's "generosity" later. Or maybe it is designed to reinforce you putting their needs ahead of your own. The point is that the narcissist's gestures of kindness come with ulterior motives.

The awareness you had of your narcissistic parent's ulterior motives may make it difficult to trust others' expressions of kindness toward you. There is an overlap between the narcissist's occasional kind gesture and someone else's sincere gesture. From the outside, they can look very similar. The way you learned to survive such acts of kindness can make it hard to trust and take in a sincere act of kindness shown to you by someone safe today.

Many survivors of narcissistic abuse had to steel themselves inside whenever their narcissistic abuser showed kindness toward them. They describe knowing that it was a setup and that the risk lay in letting their guard down to take in the narcissist's kindness. If they did, the person from whom they accepted the kindness would later accuse them of being inconsiderate, inadequate, inferior, etc. If they had let themselves stay open to and believe the initial kindness, the resulting accusations and character attacks would only have hurt that much more. So, it was with a measure of grit and wisdom that the survivor learned to go rigid inside at these times so as not to take the bait. If this inner experience resonates with you, I hope you can offer yourself some credit for what you managed to do in such a dire situation.

Three Tools to Facilitate Trust After Narcissistic Abuse

And now for the challenge (or opportunity) facing survivors once they have distanced themselves enough from their narcissistic abuser and are in relationships where someone is offering them sincere kindness. The same tactic that saved your psychological and emotional self from the narcissistic abuser's attempts to set you up can interfere with taking in the real thing from other people. Here are a few tools to help repurpose the strategies that have served valiantly to protect you in the past and trust the new, sincere feedback offered by the right people:

- **Put distance between yourself and your narcissistic abuser.** We cannot drop our weapons when the war is still going on. It is imperative to get psychological, emotional, and physical distance from the narcissistic abuser before working to trust others' good intentions. Dropping your guard when your abuser is still around can result in the exact wounding you've worked so hard to protect yourself from.

- **Find safe relationships.** One feature of safety is the that the person reflects back who you are to them and how and why you matter. It does not have to be stated overtly—it can be conveyed through attitude and action, too.
- **Watch, track, and when necessary, challenge the meanings you make of these safe people's kindness toward you.** For example, if a friend invites you to dinner, you might check your inner monologue and examine why you think they want your company. If a part of you believes they feel obligated or are just trying to seem like a welcoming person, this might reflect what would have been true with the narcissistic abuser. Try to think of and try out alternative understandings, such as: *I am a valued friend, and this person wants to spend more time with me because they care about me.*

These alternative understandings may not—in fact, probably will not—feel believable at first. As with so much in this recovery process, just because something feels unfamiliar doesn't mean it's less accurate than what feels familiar.

40

Know You Are Adequate

> *Did it feel very dangerous to entertain any positive thought about yourself around your narcissistic parent? Does it seem like feeling good about yourself will result in something catastrophic? Does it seem impossible to have a relationship where both people feel good about themselves?*

A narcissistic parent's efforts to relocate their own sense of worthlessness into a scapegoated child can create a confusing and hurtful self-concept for that child. In this chapter, I explain why it can be forbidden for the scapegoat child to know they are adequate while in relationship to the narcissistic person. There are two reasons for this—the demands of the narcissistic abuser and the scapegoat child's need to feel attached. I will offer a case example that embodies this. Last, I will emphasize the importance of challenging the belief that you are inadequate in relationships with safe people.

> *Greg was in his early thirties and came to treatment complaining of self-sabotage when he seemed to be on the*

brink of successes at his job. As we talked more, it became clear that he did not suffer from a lack of work ethic. In fact, Greg always seemed to be structuring his time so that he was working toward some goal or another. He told me the idea of not working toward something filled him with feelings disgust.

As we continued to work in therapy, Greg described how he was frequently attacked by his narcissistic father, and that he could always be sure it would happen if he was in a state of rest. He recalled one time when he had gotten a root canal on several of his teeth, and per the dentist's orders, he'd taken the afternoon off from his summer job as a furniture mover. The work in the heat was intense, and he had been relieved to have the day off.

His narcissistically abusive father walked into the room where Greg was lying down and asked him what he was doing. When Greg explained that he was resting from the root canal, his father went ballistic and told him to get his work clothes on immediately and go back to work, and that he was being self-indulgent and lazy by trying to skip work for this "BS reason." Greg had no choice, and with his head throbbing as the pain medication wore off, he spent the rest of the day moving heavy furniture. He said that going to work was better than accepting his father's accusations of how inadequate he was for resting.

Greg's father would also incessantly harass him. The message he received was that he was inadequate and always try to prove otherwise. Whether it was for putting silverware in the dishwasher the wrong way, or failing to bring a permission slip home to get signed for a field trip, or not knowing how to do a task that he'd never done before, his father would yell at and attack Greg's character. But the core attitude of his father was that Greg—as a person—was inadequate. This was evident in how his father curiously never gave credit him for his obvious adequacies. He was a very good student, but his father would accuse him of being lazy at school. He was an empathic person who was well-liked, but his father would say that he knew how to "tell people what they wanted to hear."

Greg wanted to live from a sense of his own adequacy, and he wanted therapy to help him with this goal. We discussed how he would feel deeply inadequate when he was at rest in one way or another. It was clear that he had come by these feelings as a result of his father's treatment. If Greg was at work or engaged in an activity after work or on the weekends, he could feel reasonably OK about himself. As soon as he had free time, however, he would feel like he was sinking into an internal abyss of inadequacy. He realized that he'd never experienced the feeling of a job well done, despite having done many jobs quite well in his life.

This is where therapy worked to help Greg gain insight into the origins of this feeling of inadequacy. Eventually Greg changed the definition of his problem. His problem was not that he hadn't yet done enough to prove his adequacy as a person. His problem was that he held the faulty assumption that he was inadequate to begin with. I was helpful in this regard, expressing how differently he saw and experienced Greg compared to how his father had treated him. I saw and treated him as someone who deserved respect, was worthy of admiration for his actual traits, and was fundamentally a good and adequate person. As Greg grew more accustomed to being treated in the way he deserved to be, he was able to more clearly see how his father had managed his own deep sense of worthlessness by finding Greg to be the inadequate one. Eventually, Greg was able to be compassionate toward himself for having had to believe in his inadequacy as the only way to stay attached to his narcissistically abusive father. He knew it had been more necessary for him as a boy to have someone, even if that someone treated him horribly, than to have no one at all.

By the end of therapy, Greg could afford himself many more times in his life when he did "a whole lot of nothing" without feeling inadequate. He carried around a sense of himself that felt more true, a sense that he was a capable man who expected to be treated as such by the people in his life. This new expectation helped him select and cultivate relationships with people who did, in fact, treat him this way.

Greg's case highlights how a narcissistically abusive parent can work to find the scapegoat child inadequate. It also shows why the child often has to buy into the parent's message, and highlights the elements needed to disconfirm this belief of inadequacy.

It is a fundamental truth for humans that our first priority as children is having someone there. Next is feeling good about who we are. If we cannot secure a bond with a caregiver, our feelings about ourselves will get used in the effort to create some sort of bond. This was evident in Greg's case, but it also points to how this experience can be recovered from. In therapy, it became obvious that he was not the way his father had treated him as being. Greg was able to learn that the security of his relationship to his therapist did not depend on him feeling inadequate, the way his relationship with his father had. This was a process that took some time. Eventually, Greg could feel good about himself in an important relationship.

The Importance of Safe People in Knowing Your Adequacy

The importance of forming new, safe relationships cannot be overstated here. Therapy is one way to do this. It can allow you to gain insight into all the ways the required assumption of your inadequacy might be operating in your life. Finding good, safe people as friends and partners is another way to get to know that you can now feel good about who you are and expect continued connection to others. It does not have to be one or the other anymore.

41

Learn How to Talk to Others About a Narcissistic Parent

> *Do you struggle with situations where people who knew your narcissistic parent think highly of them?*
> *Do you worry about others reacting with disbelief and invalidation if you speak the truth about how your narcissistic parent treated you?*
> *Do you feel doubtful that anyone would support you if you told them how things were for you as a scapegoat child?*

So you've done a ton of work to recover from your narcissistic parent's abuse of you. You live with a hard-earned awareness of the truth about your parent. Now let's say you encounter someone you grew up with—a longtime friend from high school. This friend only saw the charming façade your parent showed to those outside the family. This friend asks you how that parent is doing and tells you how much they always liked him or her. What do you do?

On the one hand, making the choice to inform this person about how this parent behaved behind closed doors with you may seem most honest. On the other hand, you may not be sure how they will treat this information. Will they believe you if their experience of your parent was different? Furthermore, if you smile and nod, are you helping your narcissistic parent keep their lie going?

This chapter was inspired by a comment from my YouTube channel. A viewer named Basilrose put it this way:

"Please do a video on how to get through to friends who only knew the charming persona of a narcissistic abusive parent, and cannot fathom the need that survivors have as adults to be believed about what was happening behind closed doors when they were growing up. We don't want to walk away from these long-time friends, but it creates a rift when they don't believe our stories that contradict their own experience of the person they think they "know." It makes it even trickier when the abusive parent has passed away, a friend's reluctance to "talk badly" of the dead . . . "

I have found this concern to be common in therapy with survivors and in the Facebook group that accompanies my online course on recovering from narcissistic abuse. Basically, how do you do what's best for you and your recovery when a friend who knew your narcissistic parent presents a glowing picture of them?

In this chapter, I describe this conflict in more detail. Next, I reframe it as a question of self-care and boundaries for yourself. Last, I offer a way to counter fears of retaliation for establishing your boundaries. You can ask yourself what sort of response you want from those close to you when you share your experience with them. You get to decide whether others offer you the kind of response you deserve—or not.

Narcissistic Parents Often Present a Different Picture to the Public

A narcissistic parent often cultivates a magnanimous persona to people outside the home. As the scapegoat child, you may have had to compartmentalize your experience along the same lines. Scapegoat survivors may have experienced their narcissistically abusive parent attack them ruthlessly when they were alone, then turn around and give the world a charming smile at the drop of the hat.

In order to stay bonded to the parent, the child in this position may have had to create a similar partition within themselves. On one side of this partition was the "good" narcissistic parent, who was charming and charismatic when being observed by outside parties. On the other side of the partition was the "bad" narcissistic parent, who mercilessly berated, belittled, and devalued you when they knew they could get away with it. It may have been adaptive to keep the bad parent behind the partition in your own mind, preventing you from feeling tormented by the knowledge of the sort of person you were dependent on. In essence, you may had create a sort of "behind closed doors" experience of this parent in yourself. This may have protected you from knowing just how dangerous your parent was when you had no option to escape them.

Bring the "Bad" Parent out from behind the Closed Doors of Your Own Mind

These moments point to an opportunity to bring the bad parent out from behind the closed doors in your own mind and in the minds of others. This situation can only be experienced as an opportunity when you have accrued enough of a sense of safety in your recovery process. This happens when you have forged enough psychological and emotional distance from the narcissistic abuser and, most importantly, established relationships with safe people who readily believe and support you in your experience. You need to have traction in the three pillars of recovery, along with a sense of connection to others who have your back. With this traction in hand, you might now regard this situation as an opportunity to break down the secrecy that the narcissistically abusive parent cultivated around their mistreatment of you.

What might this look like? You could experiment with saying something like, "I had a very different experience of _____. They showed a very different side to me than they showed to people outside the home."

Choosing to respond in this manner to a friend who has a different impression of your narcissistic parent allows you to gauge that friend's response and assess whether they fit with your definition of safe others. If someone is immediately incredulous, disbelieving, or dismissive of your comment, how do you want to make sense of that information? If they show compassion and remorse at the treatment you had to endure, how do you want to make sense of that information? If they glibly change the subject and don't address your comment, then what? You get to use all of this information to assess their capacity to be the kind of friend you want in your life—or not.

It is very important to shift the frame from whether you—the survivor—will be believed by the friend to whether this friend will respond in a way that you find helpful. You are not auditioning for someone else's acceptance of your reality. You are seeing whether this person belongs among those you want to keep close to you. This is why it is so important to come at this challenge after having gained traction in your recovery. At this point, you can consider your own judgments of others rather than just their judgments of you.

If your friend comes up short in how they respond to you, you might consider limiting how close you get to them. Although this person may not be ill intentioned, their inability to provide an experience you need to feel safe with them indicates that they might not meet your personal criteria for being a safe person. This understanding may seem overly punitive. You may question whether you are being too picky or intolerant of others. You might also anticipate a wave of dread over a feared retaliation along these lines—something along the lines of, "How dare you write me off for having a different opinion than you?" These thoughts and fears are very understandable. When valuing yourself constituted a threat to your survival, it was necessary to disavow your needs. By putting your needs in the center of your life now, you are charting new territory for yourself. Your system may take some time to adjust to know it is now safe to do this.

42

Protect Your Right to Success

> *Have you found yourself in friendships or relationships where you always seemed to be the butt of the joke?*
> *Has it seemed impossible to you that such friends or partners might actually be jealous of you?*
> *Do you find yourself taking a lot more teasing than you dish out to others?*

In this chapter, I explain how getting used to the way a narcissistic parent treats you as inferior can make it hard to detect when others put you down. It may seem even more outlandish that someone else feels jealous or envious of what you possess as a person. Then I discuss the importance of protecting yourself from narcissistic abuse, paying particular attention to a common obstacle to such protection: that you may have had to take emotional care of the people who react with jealousy toward you. Last, I offer a way to assess who reacts safely to your successes and who doesn't. This tactic can help you determine who it is safe to be your good, impressive, and full self around without fear of evoking their jealousy.

When Feeling Put Down Is Familiar

As the scapegoat child, being close to the narcissistic parent typically means being made to feel inferior to that parent. The narcissistic parent will erode the scapegoat child's confidence and sense of empowerment so that they can artificially inflate their self-worth at the expense child. Devaluation often happens when the child possesses a trait, attitude, or attribute that makes the narcissistic parent aware of their own deficiency.

When this happens, the narcissistic parent will feel envy brought on by seeing someone else have what they do not. Next, they will feel a contemptuous desire to destroy what that other person has.

Having a trait, talent, or strength coveted by the narcissistic parent puts the scapegoat in danger. The child may realize that embracing such features endangers them and, to survive, learn to see themselves as deficient in this area in order to dampen their parent's envy. This is why a physically attractive scapegoat child can believe that they are hideous, or an extremely intelligent scapegoat child can believe they are stupid, or a kind and loving scapegoat child can believe themselves to be selfish. All of these contortions help them appear dispossessed of the attribute that evoked the narcissistic parent's envy.

When the Scapegoat Child Is Met with Envy Outside of the Narcissistic Family

Many who were scapegoated by a narcissistic parent report being in friendships and relationships where they are treated poorly. In therapy when I hear of such instances, it often seems clear that these friends or partners were envious of what the scapegoat survivor possessed. The survivor may have a hard time entertaining the idea that others wanted what they had, as they have often convinced themselves that they are bereft of value. Without intervention, this may lead the scapegoat survivor to find and maintain friendships and relationships where they feel devalued and believe they deserve it.

> *Jason came to therapy to recover from being treated as the scapegoat to a narcissistic father, who would constantly ridicule and put him down for being weird, stupid, and weak. In contrast to his father's claims, Jason was extremely bright and athletic, both as an adolescent and an adult.*
>
> *Jason remembered a friend he'd had, Dave, who would always be ready with a mocking comment toward him. If Jason started a game in football, Dave would laugh and say, "Boy, they must really be in need of players if they had to resort to you." If he did well in school, it might be, "I cannot believe you got an A on that test . . . Must be because you kiss up to the teacher so much."*
>
> *It was not until Jason was in therapy that he could consider the idea that Dave might have envious of Jason's athletic talent and intelligence. After a few months in therapy, being treated with respect and growing in trust toward his therapist, he was able to safely consider this explanation.*

Protect Yourself from Others' Envy and Devaluation

If you are a scapegoat survivor and encounter people who put you down, an important part of recovery is protecting yourself from such treatment. A crucial part of this is recognizing that you have the things that were once dangerous to possess when under the reign of your narcissistic parent. This, too, is a process. If you've spent years convincing yourself that you are not kind, smart, attractive, and so on, it will take some time and patience to entertain the opposite idea.

You can facilitate your own realization of the attributes you possess by moving away from friends and partners who react with envy to your possession of yourself. If you find yourself reluctant to share a success with a friend or partner, this may signal that they feel threatened by you being your whole self. In contrast, if you feel welcomed and celebrated when you share good news, these may be the types of people to move toward.

One obstacle that can get in the way of moving away from those who envy you is feeling responsible for their emotional well-being. There is a fragile quality to people who envy others in this manner, and for the scapegoat survivor who has a lot of empathy, this fragility can evoke a protective instinct. I would argue that in these cases, the scapegoat survivor's empathy toward such envious people comes at the cost of the survivor's own emotional well-being.

Recovery involves making yourself your priority in this regard. If you feel guilty for moving away from a someone who puts you down for being your full self, then you have a choice. You can move back toward the person who devalues you to relieve your guilt—or you can compassionately reassure yourself that you are not responsible for their well-being. Many people who are narcissistic do not take this responsibility to care for themselves and feel entitled to have others care for them in this manner. Some of the guilt felt by the scapegoat survivor may reflect a concern for what will happen to the other person when their entitled demands are not complied with. This is all to say that moving away from such people is a useful way to defy the narcissist's rules in your recovery.

43

Decide How You're Spoken To

> *Did your narcissistic parent claim your so-called bad behavior justified their bad behavior toward you? Did your narcissistic parent always seem to be the victim of your supposed insensitivity or disrespect? Do you often fear that any mistake you make could result in getting yelled at, or worse?*

This chapter addresses a destructive tactic used by the narcissistic parent and how you can begin to heal and live in defiance of it.

> *Terence came to therapy in his early thirties to recover from growing up with a narcissistic mother. She would yell and berate him for the slightest supposed offenses throughout his childhood. After divorcing his father when Terence was eleven, she could not seem to hold on to relationships or friendships. In contrast, Terence was a genuine and likable kid who had no trouble making friends in school and sports.*
>
> *However, Terence's natural buoyancy and vitality slowly eroded as he grew up under his mother's reign. It seemed to him that she would grow angry and intent on hurting him*

whenever he so much as showed up in her line of sight. In therapy, he described knowing it was a matter of when, not if, she found something he had failed to do around the house and erupted into a screaming tirade at him. His protests of innocence or that her reaction was disproportionate only seemed to make her more furious. "How can you possibly defend your deplorable actions?" she asked him rhetorically. Suffice it to say, there was no reasoning with his mother to get her to speak to him more civilly. Instead, Terence had to become hypervigilant and self-conscious to avoid doing or saying anything that would set her off. This never worked, however. It was like she was determined to find fault in him. She seemed to want an excuse to unleash her hostile aggression.

If Terence's story sounds familiar to you, then, first of all, I am sorry. I wish it didn't. Secondly, in this chapter I discuss how you can protect yourself from this type of abuse today. I describe how you can challenge the premise that your supposed misdeeds justify someone else's abusive behavior toward you.

You now have mobility in the company you keep, whereas before, you didn't. Furthermore, you can decide that the way you are spoken to counts as a criterion for whom you want to keep in your life and whom you want to move away from. You can stop worrying about whether you have done something to make someone else mad at you. Such worries can license the other person to berate and belittle you. Instead, you can ask yourself whether the person is speaking respectfully to you regardless of what you have or have not done.

How a Narcissistic Parent Offends from the Victim Position

If you have been on the receiving end of a narcissistic parent's abusive language, emotionality, and physical attack, you may have had to live by a misbegotten set of rules. These started with an asymmetrical relationship where you may have found yourself more dependent on the narcissistic parent than they were on you, as is natural between a parent and child. This starting point ensured that your main objective was to keep the relationship going. Walking away was not an option, because you needed your parent too much to do without them.

The narcissistic parent will use you—the scapegoat child—in ways that allow them to offload their feelings of worthlessness and coercively influence you to adopt them as your own. And here's an important way a narcissistic parent will do this: offend from the victim position. They will blame you for committing a supposedly unpardonable offense. Maybe you were so "thoughtless" as to not take the trash out "like they asked you to." Or maybe they accuse of responding to them in a tone of voice that they claim is "disrespectful." The narcissistic parent will claim that your bad behavior justifies their bad behavior, perhaps saying something like, "I wish you weren't so bad so I wouldn't have to yell at you like this."

In this situation, the scapegoat child's only option is to work extremely hard to avoid the initial (trumped-up) "offense." Such avoidance gives the child hope that the narcissistic parent cannot use these offenses to excuse their abusive behavior. This adaptive move lets the child survive an otherwise hopeless situation. They are left constantly worrying about the parent's happiness. They have to be ready for extreme disrespect and humiliation if the parent decides they have failed to make them happy enough. In this way, the child has to presume guilt and be proven innocent in almost every exchange with the narcissistic parent.

Nobody would assume this strategy if they enjoyed equal power to the other person. It only happens when someone in a less powerful position has to keep the other person favorably inclined toward them at all costs. In these situations, if the child were to prize their right to feel respect from the narcissistic parent over their need to have a parent who seems willing to take care of them, the child could perish—whether psychologically or physically. It is a luxury they cannot afford.

So much of recovery from narcissistic abuse boils down to incrementally learning and eventually knowing that you can do what once would have spelled your doom. The scapegoat child tried to prevent the narcissistic parent from having reasons to get angry with them. The task in recovery for the scapegoat survivor is to accrue experience that tells you it is now survivable to put your rights first in relationships.

How You Can Choose the Way You Are Treated Now

You might practice rehearsing the fact that nothing you do or do not do warrants anyone to mistreat you today. Further, if someone mistreats you for any reason, you have the right to remove yourself from the situation. And if and when you exercise your right to be treated only in ways you find acceptable, you can report these moments to the people you trust in your life. Doing so can reinforce that you are now allowed and supported in your efforts to protect yourself—without exception. By rehearsing and practicing your right to be spoken to in the manner you see fit, you can break the bind that used to tell you that one wrong move could mean you would be shamed and devalued. There are no "wrong moves" that warrant being mistreated anymore.

44

Recover Your Status

> *Are you accustomed to feeling like the least important person in group settings?*
> *Do you assume that your ideas and opinions are less valid than others'?*
> *Do you find it difficult to feel equal status in close relationships?*

If you have survived narcissistic abuse, you likely felt like you were singled out and treated with unbridled contempt and devaluation. One of the worst parts about this kind of abuse—or any form of bullying—is how the narcissist regards you as lower status than him or her. It this assumption that permits them to treat you poorly without concern. Once the narcissistic abuser sees you as lower status, your opinion of them ceases to matter. They are now free to heap as much scorn and contempt upon you as their psychopathology requires. For the scapegoat survivor of such abuse, the knowledge that the narcissist saw them as someone whose opinion didn't matter is particularly galling. Survivors may experience a gut-wrenching anger at such dehumanizing treatment.

In this chapter, I explain how the narcissist's regarding you as lower status had absolutely nothing to do with the status you deserve in this world. Next, I provide examples of how a scapegoat child is influenced to think of themselves as lower status than the narcissistic parent. Last, I offer a strategy to help you escape the trap of trying to prove your status to yourself. Instead, you can assume the equal status to others that you've deserved all along. This can allow you to recover your status after narcissistic abuse.

Why It Is Necessary for the Narcissist to See You as Lower Status

AS I have discussed, narcissists try to cope with their core sense of worthlessness by denying this feeling and insisting the opposite to themselves—that they are in fact more special and important than others. Unfortunately, since denial is never a very viable strategy, those feelings of worthlessness do not disappear. The narcissist now needs to find someone else—usually someone over whom they have authority, like a child—to relocate these feelings into.

In order to do this, the narcissist needs the scapegoat child and other family members to agree with the scapegoat's lower status. Without such agreement, the narcissistic parent's mistreatment of the child may not be seen as something the child deserves. This is where undermining the scapegoat child's status in the family comes into play. The narcissistic parent—the most powerful member of the family—"finding" their own worthlessness in the scapegoat child implicitly communicates that the scapegoat child is of lower status than everyone else in the family.

When other members of the family perceive the scapegoat child to be of lower status, there can be a sense of superiority and relief that it is the scapegoat child and not them who is the focus of the narcissist's devaluation.

The Impact of Being Seen as Lower Status for the Scapegoat Child

I think the most painful part of being deemed lower status than the narcissist is their lack of care about what the child thinks about them. This is a devastating blow for anyone in relationship to someone else. The fundamental glue that holds two people together is a mutual caring and respect for what they think of each other. Each person values the other enough for the other's evaluation to matter to them. This prevents one person from acting abusively toward the other, because they do not to be seen as mean or cruel by them.

The scapegoat child does not have this glue in the relationship with the narcissistic family. They do not see the child as possessing enough status to care what that child thinks of them. The narcissistic parent and enabling family members are free to treat the child terribly without consequence. The scapegoat child may seethe with indignation at how they always seem to be against him, but his protest will not be taken seriously.

Importantly, the claim that the scapegoat child is of lower status than the rest of the family is pure fiction. It's just not true. Scapegoat survivors of such treatment often speak of having had to swallow an identity that always felt wrong, yet that was pushed upon them and reinforced over and over by their family. Like the pin of a membership badge being pushed into the skin of the scapegoated child, it hurts when it goes in, yet cannot be taken off if the child is going to stay in the family.

How to Recover Your Status

Put another way, how does one fight a lie? It can be a trap to try to prove to the original accusers that they are wrong. Doing so lends too much legitimacy to their initial claims that you were lower status. When you protest this framing of your identity, you risk giving it more credence than it deserves. There are a lot of examples of this principle in popular culture—a person says something about another person, and when that person tries to defend themselves, it only reinforces in everyone's mind that there was something to the initial accusation.

With that understanding in hand, the next step is to gain psychological, emotional, and perhaps physical distance from the person or system insisting that you are lower status. This, to me, is equivalent to freeing yourself from a Chinese finger trap. This contraption is a woven tube of bamboo shoots where you stick your two index fingers in on either sides of the tube, and the harder you pull your fingers out, more the tube tightens around them. If you push your fingers deeper into the tube, however, it widens and you're able to pull your fingers out. Getting distance from the narcissistically abusive person or group that insists on your lower status is a lot like doing the counterintuitive thing with the finger trap that actually leads to a solution. Instead of trying to prove to the narcissistic abuser that you are of equal status, you are walking away, allowing them to think or claim whatever they like. In the meantime, the stress of knowing you are being regarded as lower status is absent and figures less and less prominently in your experience of yourself and your own life.

With enough time and distance from your narcissistic abuser, you can begin to live as if you are of equal status to others. This may be unfamiliar to scapegoat survivors of narcissistic abuse, and as such, it can be useful to just pay attention to what it feels like to assume your equal status. As you live in this manner and assume that your point of view, ideas, and preferences are as legitimate as others', you may experience a sense of acceptance and appreciation for who you uniquely are and what you bring to the world. It may take some time to get to that point. I encourage you to exercise patience and compassion toward yourself as you do this.

45

Trust What the Narcissist Shows You, Not What You Hope to See

> *Is it hard to believe that your own parent mistreated you?*
> *Do you often doubt your perceptions of your narcissistic parent and wonder if you are being too hard on them?*
> *Do you assume that others will think you are wrong if you tell them how you felt in relation to your narcissistic parent?*

Scapegoat survivors of narcissistic abuse often find it very difficult to take the narcissist's behavior toward them at face value. This makes sense. As a child, the relationship to the narcissistic parent had to be more important than the scapegoat child's own well-being. The child didn't have the option of trusting what the narcissistic parent was showing them. Who else did they have to go to? Instead, the scapegoat child had to come up with elaborate mental games that afforded sympathy toward the narcissistic parent.

In the process of recovery from such abuse—whether in therapy or in nurturing friendships and relationships—the survivor grows to trust that there are alternate sources of connection for them. Now it can seem possible that they can feel good, protected, and respected with other safe people. As these new experiences and relationships take root, the scapegoat survivor finds it easier to take the narcissistic parent's behavior toward them at face value. Now the survivor gets to prioritize how *they* felt in relation to the narcissistic parent instead of thinking about the rationale for why the narcissist may have felt compelled to treat them this way. The scapegoat survivor is empowered to trust the behaviors that other people show them. They can then more reliably populate their lives with people who consistently behave toward them in ways that make them feel accepted and like things are running well.

In this chapter, I discuss the challenge of trusting what a narcissist shows you when you are dependent on that narcissistic person. Next, I discuss how to shift your priority from the narcissistic parent's well-being to your own. Last, I emphasize the importance of longstanding, close, and supportive relationships with new, safe people to make this shift.

The Self-Centered World of Narcissistic Parenting

Sometimes when a scapegoat survivor reflects on how a narcissistic parent mistreated them, they find themselves thinking sympathetically about the "plight" of their parent. This can drown out their own experience and suffering. Scapegoat survivors may say things like, "I really don't think they intended to hurt me so badly" or "They had a really bad childhood themselves and did not know any different." Now the scapegoat survivor is caught wondering more about the narcissist's intentions and history than their own well-being.

This makes good psychological sense. If you are a child to a narcissistic parent, you are also biologically motivated to preserve the bond to that parent. Someone who is pathologically narcissistic is fundamentally incapable of fulfilling their end of this bargain. Such an individual has to devote all of their psychological and emotional energy to keeping their inflated yet very fragile self-esteem intact. This mission shifts what other people are for. Instead of other people being potential opportunities for bonding, they are solely sources of admiration, subjects to be controlled, or reflections of the narcissist's superiority. Psychologically speaking, a relationship with a narcissist is all about that person. The child born to a narcissistic parent learns that feeling connected to that parent means making the parent the center of their world—instead getting to be the center of their own world.

The scapegoat child has to sacrifice themselves for the sake of a relationship. Healing from narcissistic abuse takes place in the context of new, safe relationships. Therapy is one form of such a safe relationship. In my work as a therapist, I listen for vestiges of this initial sacrifice that the child of a narcissistic parent has had to make. One of the main ways that the sacrifice of the self can live on is in the topic discussed here: the focus on the narcissistic parent's reasons or hardships that led to their abusive behavior toward the survivor. When this happens, I do whatever I can to empower the survivor to focus on how *they* felt in relation to the narcissist rather than the person's intentions or history.

Scapegoat survivors often find it radical to consider that they can base their conclusions about another person—including a narcissistic abuser—on how they feel in relation to that person. Most scapegoat survivors have had their own reality questioned, undermined, and invalidated so much that their own feelings do not feel like they're "enough" to base conclusions upon. Instead, they've had to do mental gymnastics to justify the narcissistic parent's malevolent perspective of them, at the cost of possessing themselves.

An even more profound shift can happen when survivors move the narcissist out of the center of their own worlds in favor of themselves. Doing so makes the realm of relationships depend on what others show you rather than who they are in an abstract sense. A survivor of narcissistic abuse often has to think of other people as ideas, because the actual people in their lives were too painful to know. So, a survivor's narcissistic mother becomes an abstracted idea of "mom," whom the survivor thinks of as smiling and good to people. This same mother might change to berating and yelling at the survivor for some supposed offense behind closed doors. When this happened, the survivor would feel trapped, humiliated, and deathly afraid.

These feelings and the information contained therein could not be known by the survivor while living under the same roof as their narcissistic parent. Instead, the survivor had to think of his mother in this idea-based way but could not know who she was to him based on how she made him feel. There is a difference between the thinking that the child of a narcissistic parent has to do to keep the faith that they have a parent who is good to them versus knowing how someone else makes them feel and whether their entire organism is drawn to or repelled by them.

Unlearning the Narcissist: Empowering Yourself after Abuse

When a scapegoat survivor gets to identify and challenge the mandate to put the other person at the center of their worlds, then they get to know how other people make them feel and make decisions based on this information. The survivor gets to gradually think about the ways their narcissistic parent treated them as wrong because they felt wrong. There is way less of a felt demand to justify feeling wounded by answering all of the imagined counterarguments the narcissist might have if they saw you putting yourself first in this way. Retorts like, "Oh, you're being too sensitive," or "See? You are the narcissistic one, always making everything about yourself," or "When are you gonna get over it? You're just stuck in the past." The volume of these imagined rebukes gets turned down so low that the survivor stops even acknowledging them. Meanwhile, the volume has been turned up on what they do and do not want for themselves.

The goal is to care more about your own feelings than those of the narcissist. That takes time, compassion with yourself, and patience. Most importantly, it happens in the context of new, safe relationships. Whether in therapy or elsewhere, this repositioning of yourself in the center of your life can only happen in the context of a new relationship. A survivor has to accrue new relational experience that tells them it is now safe to put themselves in the center of their lives, and that doing so does not evoke rebuke, rejection, or abandonment by the other person.

Instead, the survivor may find appreciation, positive regard, and generosity of spirit.

Why are such new relationships a critical ingredient to the process of recovery? It strikes at the heart of the trauma suffered by the survivor of narcissistic abuse. The survivor learned to fear the loss of their relationship to the narcissist more than the narcissist's mistreatment of them. Actions that would make the survivor feel good would threaten the narcissist's fragile sense of superiority, and so had to be avoided. In recovery, the attempt to center oneself can post-traumatically feel like it is going to lead to abandonment or rejection, just like it used to with the narcissist. So, the survivor needs to be able to take these actions on their own behalf and then experience the continued presence of the other safe person still benignly being there.

Overcoming Anxiety: The Path to Self-Assertion

This process is similar to the exposure and response prevention method used with those who suffer from obsessive-compulsive disorder. (OCD). When someone is obsessively afraid of contamination and touches a doorknob, they may wash their hands compulsively to relieve their resulting anxiety. Exposure and response prevention works by having a therapist accompany the person when they touch a doorknob and resist the urge to wash their hands. As they tolerate their anxiety without doing what—temporarily—relieves it, their system gets to learn that nothing catastrophic will happen when they touch the doorknob. It can take a while before this conclusion is drawn, and a fair amount of anxiety may need to be endured. However, the results can be well worth it.

For the scapegoat survivor, the exposure is to acts of self-assertion. These acts are akin to the OCD sufferer touching the doorknob. A survivor may be inclined to do the equivalent of handwashing by criticizing themselves or otherwise putting themselves down in order to alleviate the anxiety that results from putting themselves first. Something therapeutic happens when they assert themselves in a safe relationship and feel less anxiety due to the other person's receptive response. Instead of criticizing themselves to reduce their anxiety, they see what happens with the other person.

46

Show Off

> *Were you often told that expressions of pride were "bragging"?*
> *Did your narcissistic parent withhold affirmation or actively shame you for expressing pride?*
> *Did your narcissistic parent treat you like you had nothing to be proud about?*

I remember that my favorite days in elementary school were then ones when we got to do show-and-tell. These were days when the teacher would devote thirty minutes for our class to sit in a circle, and each student got a turn to show some item or skill that they wanted to tell the class about. These days at school offered a safe way to tap into something I liked about myself and know that it was expected and appropriate to share that with others. There would be no accusations of bragging or showing off. Showing and telling was what I was supposed to do. Unfortunately, there are far fewer opportunities for such formal show-and-tell in adulthood.

What does show and tell have to do with recovering from narcissistic abuse for the scapegoat survivor? When living with their narcissistic abuser, scapegoat children often found it necessary to suppress the healthy desire to show and tell about themselves. Instead they had to be the appreciative audience to the narcissistic parent showing and telling. The rules at home dictated that when they engaged in show-and-tell, they were shamed for bragging. Meanwhile, when the narcissistic parent was showing and telling about themselves, it deserved applause.

In this chapter, I explain how survivors of narcissistic abuse can go to great lengths to avoid showing off in their current lives. Next, I explain the importance of showing off to the development of a healthy sense of self. Third, I describe the psychological dynamics that lead to the scapegoat survivor feeling like they are uniquely forbidden from showing off while others are permitted to. Last, I offer an exercise you can do in your life to afford yourself more moments of showing off.

Why Showing Off Feels So Bad for the Scapegoat Survivor of Narcissistic Abuse

In my work, I have found that the worst danger faced by children of narcissistic parents is when the child attempts to exercise a healthy form of entitlement. If a child acts in a way that reflects their worth, the narcissistic parent will punish the child. The punishments are usually designed to make the child regret that they ever thought they were worthwhile. The scapegoat survivor can grow to feel like showing off is a direct insult to others—not because it is but because that is how this healthy striving was reacted to by a narcissistic parent.

Carlos had a very narcissistically abusive father who cultivated a family culture of acting jilted and taken from in order to be accepted as a member. If Carlos ever felt deserving, or seemed pleased with himself, his father would single him out and make up a reason to attack his character. At one point, Carlos was mocked for the way he was smiling when he came home from school after making the varsity basketball team. Then his father shifted to berating Carlos for not cleaning up his room. In therapy, we understood that the triggering event for his father was Carlos's pride in himself. His father experienced this pride as taking away from his own exaggerated sense of self-importance.

At the start of therapy, some of the most anxiety-producing moments for Carlos were when he thought I experienced him as being too demanding. One week, he told me what he had found helpful in our previous session. I said, "Yeah, I hear you saying that you'd like to be contributed to by me sharing my thoughts with you more often in session." Carlos had been worried that I might feel insulted by him revealing that I was not perfect as a therapist. If he'd been right, I would have grown hostile and malevolent toward him for acting in such an "entitled" way toward me. The thing was, Carlos was right about everything but the last part. I thought he was exercising his entitlement to let me know what worked and did not work for him, and I was very grateful for his feedback. He allowed me to better reach the goal of our relationship feeling good for him. Carlos was used to his father's goal of using their relationship to feel better than him. We were working on a new paradigm, one where I was aware that I could never perfectly meet his needs and needed his help in telling me what worked best for him.

In this example, Carlos was showing off, in a sense, by saying what he wanted more of in session, and our work highlighted how wrongly punished he had been for doing such a healthy thing in relationship to his father. Showing off can take lots of different forms. Maybe it involves initiating a conversation about something you've achieved rather than inviting the other person to share what they are proud about in their lives. These moments of revealing oneself to others and the world are critical ones, which can help or hinder our development of a healthy sense of self.

Heinz Kohut said that kids are seeking to use their parents as good-enough mirrors for who they are in the world. When the parent responds frequently enough with empathic resonance, appreciation, and support, the child gets to identify an act of "showing off" as a signal of who they are. Over time and repetition, such interactions grow to build a positive sense of self.

For example, a three-year-old boy goes down a tall slide on the playground for the first time and lands on the ground. His father looks at him and shakes his fist in an affirming way. He is empathically resonating with the child's feeling of accomplishment. This signals to the child that what he's feeling is recognized, participated with, and valued by his father. This child might get to know that he is someone who likes to take on slightly scary activities to get the feeling of exhilaration that comes afterward. That's how a parent mirroring a kid's act of showing off can help the kid develop a healthy sense of self.

Here is how it can work with a narcissistic father: The boy gets to the bottom of the slide, and his father grabs him harshly by the arm and tells him not to do such dangerous things. Now the boy learns that showing off what he can do is met with contempt and punishment by his father. The boy is prevented from being able to use the interaction as a good reflection of who he is.

Why the Narcissistic Parent Cannot Stand Your Showing Off

The narcissistically abusive parent starts with a core sense of worthlessness that has to be relocated into others so that they can more effectively deny these feelings to themselves and insist on their opposite. It is a fragile arrangement that needs others to constantly reflect back their specialness, or the system breaks down and they are put back in touch with their intolerable feelings of worthlessness. Well, if you suffered in the role of scapegoat to someone like this, then you were the person they tried to relocate these feelings of worthlessness into. As a result, if you showed feelings of self-worth, you were not cooperating with the function the narcissist needed you to serve. If the relationship with the narcissistic abuser is asymmetrical, where the narcissist holds more authority or the scapegoat is dependent on the narcissist, then there is nothing to do but go along with being whom the narcissistic abuser needs you to be for their psychological purposes. This is why healthy efforts to show off are so roundly punished and eradicated by narcissistic parents—they threaten to put that parent in touch with the worthlessness that they insist the scapegoated child be the one to feel all the time.

47

Stop Self-Punishment

> *Do you feel low or down after periods of feeling good, proud, or effective?*
>
> *Do you feel like you have done or are doing something wrong even though you cannot point to anything?*
>
> *Do you carry around a sense that the other shoe is going to drop? That it's a matter of when, not if?*

Many survivors of narcissistic abuse report these experiences of self-punishment. In this chapter, I explain how and why self-punishment can become a survival tactic. Next, I discuss a counter-intuitive strategy to transform this habit into an experience of deeper acceptance of yourself.

Why Scapegoat Survivors Punish Themselves after Good Things Happen

Tom was a very smart, hard-working, and engaging young man. He came to therapy wanting to get over a pattern at work where he could only be productive if he felt like he was on the verge of getting fired. Once that stage was set, he worked tirelessly toward his goals. When this resulted in an inevitable promotion, he would find it very difficult to complete even basic tasks for his job. As this set in, he'd grow extremely punitive toward himself. "Why can't I just do what I know I can do?!" *he would exclaim in sessions.*

Tom had survived a narcissistic father who thought he could do nothing right. As a teenager, he told Tom he should have more friends, so Tom went about cultivating a social life for himself. Then his father would yell at him for always prioritizing his friends over his family, so Tom cut off his friendships. No matter what Tom did to try to win his father's approval, he would change the rules or move the goalposts.

Tom's situation was further complicated by the fact that his father was the more viable parent to attach to. Due to his mother's emotional volatility and general unavailability, his father was the only one present enough to offer Tom this kind of relationship. This meant that he faced the suffering-filled prospect of having to get close to someone who hurt him.

In therapy, we came to understand that Tom had found a way to get close to his narcissistically abusive father by treating himself the same way his father would treat him. This afforded him a sense of psychological nearness. As a child, he needed to feel like there was someone in the world to whom he mattered.

It also was adaptive for Tom to minimize the damage his father would do to him. He'd beat his father to the punch and appear downtrodden or unsuccessful, in essence *showing his father that he didn't have to feel threatened by Tom taking pride in his own existence.*

In adulthood, this strategy created problems for Tom when he succeeded. Success made him feel (psychologically) far away from his father, which made him feel scared—two outcomes he had avoided as a child by avoiding success. Tom's sudden difficulty doing basic job tasks after the success of being promoted helped him avoid the old remembered danger of losing someone he needed, and made him less of a target to that person. So, these difficulties operated to Tom's advantage in a certain way. However these acts of self-punishment also caused him frustration and angst in his current situation.

Tom's experience illustrates the important function of self-punishment when the job is to attach to someone who is narcissistically abusing you as the scapegoat. This strategy, as much as it may interfere with pursuing your goals and wanted experiences in life, might deserve your respect and appreciation, as it once helped you narrow life down to something that could make the unendurable endurable.

Transform the Practice of Self-Punishment

The goal is to own this part of yourself. You may understandably see your inclination to protect yourself, with self-punishment as your enemy. You might usefully work to see this part of you that deserves a relationship with yourself. That can be enough for a while. Do not ask it to change. Just be with it. "Oh, I feel this part of me that's telling me I don't deserve this promotion, or my partner is not going to be happy to see me tonight, or my friends are going to be sick of me . . ." These are all the kinds of self-punishing thoughts or states that might come up.

Instead of seeing these self-punishing thoughts and feelings as your adversaries, what if your goal was to get closer to them? Offer them your company?

Your goals for yourself and these self-punishing tactics are all a part of you. The effort to eradicate a part of oneself does not often succeed. It can often create it is own form of suffering—a sense of dissatisfaction with your inner experience. The crux of being narcissistically abused as the scapegoat survivor is that you don't feel accepted by those who are supposed to offer unconditional acceptance. By adopting an accepting attitude toward all parts of your experience, you are offering yourself an important antidote to this aspect of the abuse. This can be healing in its own right.

48

Seven Self-Care Tools to Help You Defy the Narcissist's Rules

> *Would you like a series of tactics you can use in your life to help yourself heal from narcissistic abuse? Is it sometimes difficult to know how to stay on the path toward feeling more deserving and intact? Do you at times find it challenging to keep your morale up during this process?*

The process of recovery from narcissistic abuse as the scapegoat involves learning to treat yourself in ways that are loving but probably unfamiliar. In fact, the ways you might work to treat yourself could have spelled danger when you had to maintain your narcissistic parent's goodwill toward you. Since these lessons were learned in a traumatic way—under threat of severe attack or abandonment—it will likely take time, patience, and compassion to learn new lessons. The stakes were too high when the initial lessons were learned for it to be otherwise.

In this chapter, I lay out a plan for self-care, which you can think of as a prescription for yourself. If you are prescribed medicine, it is often something you take daily no matter what. Some days you may want to take it and others you may not. But the idea is that you commit to taking the medicine to protect your health.

Acts of self-care for the scapegoat survivor may usefully be thought of as prescriptions. It may feel very difficult to do these things for yourself on a regular basis, and that's OK. You don't have to feel like doing these practices in order to do them. With repetition, you are giving yourself firsthand experience caring for yourself, learning that you deserve it even when it does not feel that way. That is an important antidote to the lessons you learned as a scapegoat.

With that said, if you miss a day, week, or month of doing these exercises, compassion toward yourself is still warranted. The legacy of narcissistic abuse is often a harsh inner critic that claims nothing you do is good enough. Giving yourself permission to do the best you can with these exercises is another way of defying the narcissist's rules.

Self-Care Tool #1: Practicing Patience with Yourself

If you've survived narcissistic abuse, you may be familiar with feeling like you are behind schedule. One of the ways a narcissistic person can influence someone to feel inadequate is to treat them as if they are slow, wrong, and/or don't know what they're doing. This can create a feeling of always being behind.

The process of recovery can fall prey to this way of thinking about yourself. It is important to counter this with deliberate efforts to grant yourself the right to take the time you need to recover. I was once told in my own therapy, when I was wondering if I could have done something earlier in life to be further along in my process of recovery, that "nothing was wasted."

Exercise: Put one hand on your chest and one hand on your lower abdomen. Take three breaths, then say to yourself: "Nothing was wasted. I am exactly where I need to be right now." Do this three times per day.

Self-Care Tool #2: Practicing Gratitude toward Yourself

In narcissistic abuse, the survivor often gets used to a near-constant state of emotional deprivation. There is an inherent inequality in the relationship to the narcissistic partner or parent, where all of the attention, respect, and gratitude typically goes toward the narcissist—or else!

This act of self-care is designed to counteract the state of deprivation you may have experienced. By identifying qualities in yourself or others and experiences you've had that you either feel grateful for or could hypothetically feel grateful for, you are building a new way of experiencing and thinking about yourself in the world. This will make you feel like you have access to—and deserve—sources of happiness in your own life.

Exercise: Every night, thirty minutes before bedtime, write down at least ten things you are grateful for today. It does not matter how big or small these things are.

Self-Care Tool #3: Use Your Breath

In the course of narcissistic abuse, the mandate is to pay more attention to the narcissist's thoughts, feelings, and well-being than your own. This can result in paying little attention to your own physiology. Survivors may find themselves automatically holding their breath and keeping their attention focused on what's going on around them rather than what's going on within.

Recovery from narcissistic abuse needs to include restoring the connection between your mind and your body. The breath can be an important catalyst for this. Whether you choose to or not, you're always breathing. The act of paying attention to your breath without doing anything to it or wanting it to change can be a powerful antidote to what you have been used to. Other ways of deliberately breathing into different parts of your body can also be helpful.

Exercise 1: For three minutes, twice a day, sit down in a comfortable position. Slowly bring your attention to your breath and just notice it. Do not breathe deeper or differently. Just notice the cadence of your breath.

Exercise 2: For three minutes, once a day—at a different time than Exercise 1—inhale through the nose for a count of four, hold that breath for a count of four, and exhale through the nose for a count of eight.

Self-Care Tool #4: Making Sure to Move

As part of the mandate to make the narcissist matter more than you matter to yourself, a sort of frozenness can overtake a person's experience. This may be adaptive when being narcissistically abused because it can shrink your awareness of your own body, experience, feelings, and thoughts. Furthermore, a victim of narcissistic abuse often has to experience shame due to the lack of relational contact offered by the narcissist. Shame is an emotion that we often cope with by freezing.

In recovery, movement becomes possible and important to practice. "Expressive meditation" is a form of movement that emphasizes spontaneity and freedom. With regular practice, you will feel more connected to your bodily rhythms and experience fewer states of freezing.

Exercise: Expressive meditation is great way to practice spontaneous movements with your body. Useful music to play in the background can be found for free on YouTube by searching for "Osho Kundalini Meditation." For at least five minutes, allow yourself to move, shake, and amble in whatever ways your body wants to. There is no wrong way to do this. Try to practice this once per day.

Self-Care Tool #5: Eating as an Act of Care toward Yourself

Recovery can be hard work, and we need to be as close to full strength as possible to undertake it. As I've discussed and written about elsewhere, one of the common beliefs held by a scapegoated survivor of narcissistic abuse is the idea that they are physically disgusting. When you are forced to adopt this belief, your relationship to food and eating can get compromised. Instead of food being something to fuel and propel you toward sources of happiness, purpose, and connection in life, it can become something that contributes to feeling more—or less—physically disgusting. This is especially the case if this belief centers on body image perceptions such as being "too fat" or "too skinny."

An important paradigm shift in eating can be to think of it as fuel for your recovery. The goal is to eat foods that allow your digestive tract, nervous system, and bodily chemistry to function optimally, not to manage or dispel a body image concern.

Exercise: Remind yourself daily that you need your body at full strength to recover from narcissistic abuse. With this in hand, patiently and gently, work to adopt these practices:

- Eat whole foods
- Make non-starchy vegetables 40-50 percent of your plate during meals
- 10 percent of plate your plate can be fruits
- Eat these proteins (in order of priority): plant protein (lentils, chickpeas), fish, eggs, poultry, red meat.

Self-Care Tool #6: The Respect Survey

One of the casualties of narcissistic abuse can be the survivor's own sense of self-respect. This is not because the survivor doesn't have a strong backbone or strength of character. Rather, the survivor may have learned that the narcissistic abuser reacted to any display of their self-respect as an act of provocation to be met with punishment and contempt. In this way, having learned to hide your self-respect from your abuser—and maybe even from yourself—speaks to the resilience of the survivor.

In recovery, it becomes possible to gradually reintroduce your own self-respect into your conscious experience. Of course, this assumes you have established enough distance from your narcissistic abuser.

Exercise: Select three trusted friends and/or family members. Text or email them and ask them to name at least two reasons they respect you. Compile their answers and write them down on a single sheet of paper. Consider getting this paper framed. Resolve to read it once before bedtime every night.

Self-Care Tool #7: How the Well-Adjusted World Sees You

In the course of narcissistic abuse, you may have had to adopt a perception of yourself that is at odds with how you are widely experienced by others in the world. Since the narcissist has to see you as being less than him or her, a lot of distortion and coercion can be leveraged to pressure you to comply with his or her view of you. This is particularly true when it feels like you must maintain a relationship to and share a reality with the narcissistic person at all costs.

In recovery, it becomes possible to entertain different perceptions of who you are and what you're like as a person. At the outset, these different notions may seem patently false or impossible. If you're used to thinking of yourself as inconsiderate, irresponsible, and/or inadequate, it can feel very unfamiliar to consider feedback from others that suggests you're considerate, responsible, and very adequate. Importantly, the old messages are familiar, but they are very uncomfortable to live with. These new—and more accurate messages—are less familiar, but more comfortable to live with. As you increase your familiarity with such new messages, they can grow to feel more true.

Exercise: Get a piece of paper. Imagine two people whom you have known in the course of your life who seemed to really like you. Imagine them having a conversation about you. Write down what you think they would say about you. Here are some topics to make sure these imaginary people cover:

- What drew them to you initially?
- What specifically is it about you that they like?
- Why do they think you're a good person?

Store this paper in a secure place and read it before bedtime each night.

In summary, these seven acts of self-care can serve as a foundation for your process of recovery. Ensuring that your needs are getting addressed in this prescriptive fashion directly contradicts the belief of being undeserving. Even if you do not feel like doing this act on a given day that is completely fine. You can try to do it anyway or wait a day until you recover motivation. You are already on the path to recovery and there is no such thing as going back to square one.

References

Benjamin, Jessica. 2013. *The bonds of love: Psychoanalysis, feminism, and the problem of domination.* Pantheon.

Buber, Martin 1970. *I and Thou* (Vol. 243). Simon and Schuster.

Celani, David. 2005. *Leaving home: The art of separating from your difficult family.* Columbia University Press.

Cloud, Henry, and John Townsend. 1996. *Safe people: How to find relationships that are good for you and avoid those that aren't.* Grand Rapids: Zondervan.

Fisher, Janina. 2017. *Healing the fragmented selves of trauma survivors: Overcoming internal self-alienation.* Routledge.

Kohut, Heinz. 2013. *The analysis of the self: A systematic approach to the psychoanalytic treatment of narcissistic personality disorders.* University of Chicago Press.

Lewin, Kurt. 1951. *Field theory in social science: selected theoretical papers* (Edited by Dorwin Cartwright.). Harpers.

Peck, M. Scott. 1983. *People of the Lie.* Simon and Schuster.

Pillari, Vimala. 1991. Scapegoating in families: Intergenerational patterns of physical and emotional abuse. New York, NY: Brunner/Mazel.

Reid, Jay, and David Kealy. 2022. "Understanding and Working with the Effects of Parental Pathological Projective Identification." *Smith College Studies in Social Work* 92, no. 2 1-18.

Rogers, Carl Ransom. 1995. *On becoming a person: A therapist's view of psychotherapy.* Houghton Mifflin Harcourt.

Schwartz, Joseph. 2015. "The Unacknowledged History of John Bowlby's Attachment Theory." *British Journal of Psychotherapy*, 31(2), 251-266.

Schwartz, Richard C., and Martha Sweezy. 2019. *Internal family systems therapy.* Guilford Publications.

Seligman, Stephen. 2018. Relationships in development: Infancy, intersubjectivity, and attachment. New York, NY: Routledge.

Silberschatz, George. 2013. *Transformative relationships: The control mastery theory of psychotherapy.* Routledge.

Tolle, Eckhart. 2004. *The power of now: A guide to spiritual enlightenment.* New World Library.

Urbonaviciute, Greta, and Erica G. Hepper. 2020. "When is narcissism associated with low empathy? A meta-analytic review." *Journal of Research in Personality*, 89, 104036.

Vogel, Ezra F., and Norman W. Bell. 1960. "The emotionally disturbed child as a family scapegoat." Psychoanalytic Review, 47(2), 21-42.

Walker, Pete. 2013. *Complex PTSD: From surviving to thriving.* Azure Coyote.

Printed in Great Britain
by Amazon